STRATEGIC PLANNING

Cases, Concepts, and Lessons

SECOND EDITION

James T. Ziegenfuss, Jr.

University Press of America,® Inc.
Lanham · Boulder · New York · Toronto · Plymouth, UK

Copyright © 2006 by
University Press of America,® Inc.
4501 Forbes Boulevard
Suite 200
Lanham, Maryland 20706
UPA Acquisitions Department (301) 459-3366

Estover Road
Plymouth PL6 7PY
United Kingdom

Library of Congress Control Number: 2006930451
ISBN-13: 978-0-7618-3562-2 (paperback : alk. paper)
ISBN-10: 0-7618-3562-8 (paperback : alk. paper)

To my Uncle Edward H. Bonekemper

for his appreciation of

printing, publishing and people

TABLE OF CONTENTS

PART THREE:
LESSONS OF PROGRESS, OUTCOMES & BENEFITS............ 131

PREFACE

Lessons of strategic planning are often best learned with personal experience. My introduction to this topic involved community-level planning with an advisory board of 30 and the simultaneous operation of some six task forces involving over 100 persons. That first planning project was driven by participation from all levels of the community.

Over the past 30 years I have worked as a staff planner and as both an internal and an external planning consultant. I have engaged in planning with private companies such as banks and with state and local governments, hospitals, public and private non-profit agencies, academic departments and with private physician practices. While working, I completed doctoral studies in Social Systems Sciences at the Wharton School of the University of Pennsylvania. Russell Ackoff, Hasan Ozbekhan and Eric Trist were all researchers and practitioners of planning—their perspectives are an obvious contribution here.

In any synthesis of concepts and practice, the "lessons learned" are an integration of academic study and professional experience. I have learned much from the writings of planners and strategists, particularly Russell Ackoff, George Steiner, Henry Mintzberg and John Bryson. I have tried to relate my experiences to their approaches in my teaching and my practice and I have cited them here because their work is the foundation of the field. My students, clients and I have benefited greatly from their willingness to reflect on what we are all doing in our organizations, formally or informally.

Since 1984 I have taught the graduate course in strategic planning at Penn State University to adult students, many of whom have already had significant planning experiences. I have learned much from my students and from executives, managers and employees as they have struggled with the challenge of planning. I especially appreciate my work at academic medical centers with two medical leaders: Drs. Julien Biebuyck at Penn State and David Longnecker at the University of Pennsylvania. From John Bolger, my client and friend, I learned much about strategic issues in banking. I would like to thank several persons for research help: Sherie Stoudt, Chris Morsink and Lara Shanabraugh and for the origninal manuscript preparation, Tom Minsker and Joette Swartz. For this edition, I especially thank Katherine Ziegenfuss Sharpe and Nidhi Daga for help with editing and cases and Steve Dahm for assistance with the manuscript preparation. I also thank Harry Gray Associates and United Technologies for permission to include their *Wall Street Journal* messages and the International Institute of Informatics and Systemics for permission to use my paper.

The organization of the book is designed to take the reader from lesson to rationale to illustration to cases for further insights. Some of the best work on the topic deserves to be included although written a decade or more ago. I hope the book's audience—executives, managers, students—will be able to use the lessons for teaching, for reflection on and analysis of personal experiences, and for redesign and continuous improvement of strategic planning. This edition includes additional lessons and more than 30 cases for use in teaching and learning.

The problems presented in some cases I experienced. In other cases, I observed boards and executives, managers and employees struggle with these issues as barriers to creating their organization's future. The illustrations are composites and do not represent any one organization. I have tried to follow some of my own planning advice by presenting the lessons in as lean and as straightforward a manner as possible. Planning design, process and outcome problems are fixable, but too infrequently do we attempt to do so. The purpose of this book is to help boards, executives, managers and employees improve their planning and strategy formation processes.

James T. Ziegenfuss, Jr.
Harrisburg, Pennsylvania

STRATEGIC PLANNING: WHY & WHAT & HOW: AN INTRODUCTION*

Consider the current state of some services, fields and industries. In health care we are now in the "organization redesign" stage seeking both to improve the performance of our current delivery system and to establish the structure for a future health care system. It is clear to administrators, physicians, patients and corporate players that the current system is dysfunctional. Do we have an approach and procedure for the redesign of our organization's future? As we struggle to find a redesign approach, we find that health care professionals are far from alone. Consider the following:

- many citizens and professional educators find American educational systems fatally flawed

- manufacturers face global competition forcing them to find new ways to organize and to produce goods for a world wide market

- bankers, once secure in their community relations and small town partnerships, are acquired and closed by mega banks

- governmental leaders at all levels find dissatisfaction with public service costs, performance and relations with citizens

- individual departments in all of our organizations ask how they can redesign to address the pressures for change

The redesign problem that is so visible in health care and education turns out to be a common problem across fields and professional disciplines. An integrated systems-oriented approach to redesign is the underlying philosophy of this book.

---

* Adapted from James T. Ziegenfuss, Jr. "Design and Redesign of the Organizational System's Future: Toward a Transdisciplinary Approach Across Work Domains." Presented at the World Multiconference on Systemics, Cybernetics & Informatics: July 12-16, 1998- Distributed in proceedings. In Ziegenfuss and Sassani (Eds.) *Portable Health Administration*. London: Elsevier/Academic Press 2004.

Imagine that one afternoon a Fortune 500 company chief executive voices his frustration with his strategic planning process. His comments to his colleague begin with:

> Mark, our process is broken. We have strategy meetings that just don't work. My people are bored at the meetings—either buried in the avalanche of background papers, or tired of taking the same positions. Our planners have given us few new ideas—and those that are new don't seem feasible to my operating managers. The executive team seems uncomfortable when we try to talk about our failures. To top it off we have too few milestones for measuring progress—although I'm not totally sure we all know where we're going.

His frustration with this often troubled managerial process is not uncommon. Strategic planning and strategy formation are ever present, absolutely needed and quite frequently flawed at large and small companies in both the private and the public sectors.

Most of us have participated in strategic planning, but our knowledge of its philosophy and our skills in practice are deficient. Here is the problem in the words of Odin Anderson.

> Planning is like the experience of a motorist who is driving on a narrow, dangerous, and winding mountain road in the rain. He chances to meet a car at a mud puddle. On passing the other car, the motorist driving up the mountain has his windshield splashed with muddy water. He turns on his windshield wiper but it does not work. Being innovative, he adjusts his rearview mirror so he can see backward as far as possible. He thereupon extrapolates where the road ahead is by watching the curves in the road behind. The moral, of course, is that this is the state of the art of planning in the health services (1).

Unfortunately this is the case in many fields, one reason for these lessons on strategy building and strategic planning.

Let's begin with the rationale for improvement. Five reasons come to mind from my own experiences in public and private organizations of all sizes and types. I expect that readers will recognize many as common to their organizations as well.

1. All successful organizations, large and small, public and private, engage in strategic planning and strategy formation. Many executives and managers feel that planning processes—to be effective—must be elaborate and complex. Others see entrepreneurial planning—quick, intuitive, action based—as the ideal. Still other executives feel that when planning is not visible it does not exist. However, experience indicates that even small organizations engage in planning, although informal and "rudimentary" in comparison to the processes of large bureaucratic organizations.

When the United Nations creates a process for visioning its future, will the process be characterized as lean and adaptive or clumsy and inflexible? Because it is responsible to many countries, employees, multiple advocacy groups, national shifts in policy simultaneously push change and lobby for status quo protection. Natural organizational behavior suggests that a bureaucratic strategy formation process will emerge at the United Nations.

2. All organizations—public and private—have less than perfect planning processes. If we are convinced that we cannot run perfect organizations, why would we expect to create perfect planning systems? In attempts to initiate planning, it is easy to be overwhelmed by the resistance presented by employees and managers. Nearly all have planning war stories to tell—negative experiences of bureaucracy, paperwork, and endless hours invested to no avail. A beginning point to the improvement journey is to admit that all organizations could create stronger planning processes, and that sometimes we make strategic mistakes.

Why did Coca-Cola get surprised by its introduction of a "new style" coke? Within the company many "discussions" were held about flawed market testing, inadequate introduction and slow remediation responses. Strategists and planners could ask what went wrong with the process.

3. All organizations—public and private—are experiencing rapidly changing environments. In years past it may have been possible to get by with a more informal and less attentive planning system. However, with new threats, opportunities and competitors, it is risky to neglect the building of organizational adaptation and flexibility. When environments change rapidly, organizations must do so as well. Planning is one way to help organizations adapt.

Changes in the business environment are visible to many executives these days. Just talk to leaders in banking and health care and to administrators of universities facing cost containment pressures on tuition. This turbulence is current. Years ago the General Electric

Boat Division faced strong defense industry cutbacks. And decades or more ago, the hostile forces of the business environment turned on the nuclear power industry, helped in part by the lack of strategic preparation for "problems" like the Three Mile Island plant in Pennsylvania. Are we really planning for changing environments?

4. All boards, executives, managers and employees should support the concept of continuous improvement of their planning systems. As more private and public organizations in the United States use the concepts of total quality management, we will be able to build support for quality improvement in the planning system. As we increase the quality of production systems, of reward systems, and of working life generally, certainly we could focus some attention on improving the quality of our planning efforts.

Some companies have become well known for embracing and successfully implementing total quality improvement. Motorola, Honda and Toyota come to mind. With "whole organization" improvement as the target, strategy planning must receive attention as well. We could even say that "improving the quality of strategic planning and strategy formation is job one."

5. All aspects of planning systems should be studied in order to improve quality. This is a somewhat simple but not obvious statement. The question is actually one of where do we start our planning improvement work? Do we begin with philosophy or with methods and techniques? What about our expectations of planning outcomes? The answer is we improve all over at once.

There is some public evidence that strategy planning systems are the subject of improvement. Years ago the media reported that GE had at one time 70 strategic planners. As a part of redesigning the planning and strategy process they reduced the number of planners to 35, tightening and redefining the role.

Given the importance of strategy and vision to private companies and public agencies, reflection on the process lessons learned seems quite logical. We are engaged in it, why not figure out what works and what does not and improve.

WHAT IS STRATEGIC PLANNING AND STRATEGY FORMATION

Mark, our chief executive, might follow-up his comments with another question: "How do strategy, strategic planning and strategy formation relate to each other?" Both academics and executives ask the same question. Our improvement efforts in this book are aimed at the more "robust" view of the strategy building process, thought to include strategic planning methods and more. We can go back to some earlier writers for fundamental premises and definitions that will give us a common frame of reference for the lessons. First, the broader view of planning extends the boundaries of the task. Planning is defined here by Professor Russell Ackoff as both strategic and "normative (2,3)."

> *Strategic planning* consists of selecting means, goals, and objectives, but ideals are either given, imposed by a higher authority, accepted by convention, or, as is usually the case, not formulated. Such planning tends to be long-range....
> *Normative planning* requires the explicit selection of means, goals, objectives and ideals. Such planning is indefinitely extended. It has no fixed horizon.

Now this definition in its combined fullness sounds much like what others have long called strategy. Consider Vancil's view:

> The strategy of an organization, *or of a subunit of a larger organization*, is a conceptualization, *expressed or implied by the organization's leader*, of (1) the long-term objectives or purposes of the organization, (2) the broad constraints and policies, *either self-imposed by the leader or accepted by him from his superiors*, that *currently* restrict the scope of the organization's activities, and (3) the *current* set of plans and near-term goals that have been adopted in the expectation of contributing to the achievement of the organization's objectives (4).

In practical terms, strategy formation is a process that aims to coordinate leaders' thinking about external and internal characteristics, the future, and the means (resources, policies, actions) for getting there. Therefore, in this book, strategic planning that includes ideals and values is the same as a broadly conceived strategy formation process.

We begin with some agreement on what strategic planning is:

- Strategic planning is a process: for understanding the present, analyzing external threats and opportunities and identifying internal strengths and weaknesses; for creating a vision of a desired future; for defining a path to the future through grand and operating strategies; and for decision making and budgeting.

The key points of the definition lead us to:

- examine outside changes of environment and competitors
- analyze our own organization's past and present performance
- create visions of the future
- select grand strategies and short term actions for moving us from the present to the future.
- link the plan to the budget

Some commentators think of strategy building and planning as design work with processes and outcomes framed in a philosophical perspective. To improve strategy building we must address both abstract and concrete issues.

In its abstract sense, strategic planning and strategy is about vision and values in the longer term future. Early advocates thought the process led to a blueprint but instead we now see strategy as a guiding framework for practical decision making. And, since corporations and public agencies are social systems, the process is group-oriented, not the production of a single individual. Although we now have some general recognition of these definitional points, there are considerable criticisms outstanding.

PHILOSOPHY AND APPROACH

By building on existing efforts to create redesigns and futures we can synthesize an approach that will transcend disciplinary boundaries and be transferable across manufacturing industries and service companies in the public and private sectors (work domains). The approach presented here is both simple and complex. It builds on three organizational improvement pillars: (1) continuous quality improvement (total quality management) (2) reengineering; and (3) vision building and strategic planning. A first example in my business —university education—illustrates the beginning notions.

Imagine three university faculty meeting for lunch to discuss the dismal state of teaching and learning. Each agrees that faculty could do much more to improve. One of the three suggests that they each make a statement of what they would do—as individuals. Their answers capture the need for an integrated approach to improvement, to radical reengineering, and to new visions.

Professor Thomas. I believe in the continuous quality improvement of our well-tested, traditional approach to teaching. I think faculty should be constantly refining and updating their lectures. In-class work should include a variety of occasional films, surprise quizzes, and regular writing requirements with detailed feedback. By continuous incremental improvement of the fundamentals, we should approximate excellence across the faculty.

Professor Franklin. I disagree. Traditional approaches have not worked. It is only through a complete reengineering of our approach to teaching will we achieve excellence. For example, I would organize the students into project teams emphasizing active learning. In-class work would include limited lecturing with much interactive "question and answer," discussion and debate. Outside work sessions would be required. Students would produce group projects and receive both individual and group grades.

Professor Martin. Wrong, we need an entirely new vision of teaching. I propose we put courses on the internet, using distance learning technologies to take courses to the student. Students would use simulations, learning much from compact disks at home. We would have a world-wide market with an international student base and self-pacing to fit individual needs (through programmed texts).

Obviously each of the professors could elaborate their individual approaches to the redesign task. This brief anecdote illustrates the three components—continuous incremental improvement of current methods, radical reengineering of classroom approaches, and a completely new vision of the educational future. All three approaches may be needed for the successful creation of the future in all of our industries and fields.

ROOTS OF THE PROCEDURAL SYNTHESIS

The combined approach is based on several common purposes. Each of the procedures—quality improvement, reengineering and visioning/strategic planning—are used for the following three purposes:

- teaching and learning
- organization change and development
- evaluation and assessment

Quality improvement work led by Deming (5), Juran (6) and Crosby (7) has been emphasizing the search for quality as an organization-wide philosophy and approach. Over the past 20–30 years, but particularly the last ten years, specific methods and tools have been developed.

Reengineering has both extended and adapted total quality management and systems thinking. Here there is a definitive emphasis on radical results—changes to core business processes. Rather than an incremental continuous improvement of existing processes, designers are asked to think of bold change. Reengineering is a "blowing up" of existing business processes (Hammer 8, Hyde 9) but not usually a redesign of the whole organization.

Ackoff's work on idealized design, first offered in the 1970's (10) takes a systems and whole-organization perspective. Participants are asked to consider the question: "if we could redesign our whole organization immediately to be more effective in this environment, what would it look like"? Rather than incremental change, this approach pushes for a radical redesign that will serve as a change incentive.

We will not further consider the history of each stream here other than to remark that their concurrent development reflects the general dissatisfaction with the status quo and the need to develop formal procedures for moving forward into a vastly changed future at both the operating level of production systems and the whole organization (culture values and grand design).

The synthesizing work can begin with any of the three streams. Here we start with Ackoff's work on idealized design because it incorporates some of the continuous improvement and reengineering thinking. In 1970, Ackoff published his approach for creating new organization designs through strategic planning processes. His

follow up works have elaborated this model over the past 25 years
(11, 12). At the same time, quality management was unfolding with
Deming, Juran and Crosby offering both the philosophy and the procedure of continuous improvement. Hammer and Champy's work
on reengineering is more recent and a derivative of these original
streams of quality improvement and new strategic vision.

ASSUMPTIONS & MODEL

All of these redesign efforts seem to point to a set of five assumptions that are the underpinnings for this presentation of a generalized
model.

1. *Redesign is sociotechnical in nature.* Organizational futures
include: (1) the *technology* or core business e.g. medical therapies,
industrial engineering, banking services (the technical aspect of
sociotechnical) and (2) the values, culture and psychology of the
workplace (the *social systems* side). Most often we think about futures in terms of new techniques and products, paying much less
attention to the nature of the social system we will need to create and
grow the business. We cannot redesign manufacturing, medical care
or teaching processes without considering the psychological impact
on providers/employees and customers.

2. *Future building is both intended/rational and emergent/intui-
tive.* We often set out to purposely plan for our desired future – an
intended, rational process. But the future of all of our organizations
"emerges" from a complex set of external environmental threats and
opportunities and internal decisions and actions (many that are intuitive and not easily explained). Thus we purposely plan *and* we
flexibly take advantage of new options and imaginative ideas. We
have moved from the grand plans—blueprints—to a sense of flexibility and adaptability based on experience. I agree with Mintzberg
that logic does not prevail over emergent creative processes (13).

3. *Redesign procedures are "rough guidance" not a mechanical
blueprint.* The most recent strategic planning and futures literature
suggests that a tight set of steps walked out in mechanical fashion is
not flexible enough to address the emergent/intuitive flow of ideas
and options that make great companies. Thus redesign should be
viewed as a "skeleton" with much room for addition, eliminating

the confinement and innovation-killing "boxes" present in many futures processes. The step-by-step procedures of the past have failed because organizational life is not so mechanized. Taken as "general direction," redesign plans help to guide us, but without detailed prescriptions.

4. Procedural adaptation is required for each unique setting— creative, innovative use of the model. Organizations are all unique. Future design processes must be created to fit each individual culture. Some are very formal and bureaucratic requiring extensive minutes and follow up reports. In others the process is informal with little written (fast moving decisions seemingly flow from "breakfast meetings"). No single model can be used in all organizations because companies and non-profits and governments are all unique enough to require tailor-made processes.

5. The model is still evolving. We are far from a consensus on a process for development of organization futures. What we are seeing is some increasing recognition of the interconnectedness of quality improvement, reengineering, visioning, and strategic planning. We have not created a definitive model of change because we are still building our knowledge of the philosophy and methods of redesign.

With these assumptions in mind, we can consider a general model of redesign in six steps.

Table 1. Model Steps

1.0 Define & Describe Present
      1.1 external conditions
      1.2 internal strengths and needs
2.0 Define & Describe Desired Future
3.0 Critical Gap Analysis
4.0 Define Grand & Leading Strategies
5.0 Identify Resource Requirements
6.0 Establish Operational Start-up: Actions, Responsibilities, & Evaluation

---

1.1 Define & Describe the Present

In order to create a redesign of an identified system—production process, department, or whole organization—we must have strong knowledge of its structures and processes and the environment in which it exists (external conditions). We begin with the external.

1.1 External Conditions. Trends and issues outside of the organization (the "environment") are scanned and analyzed as to their likely impact. The underlying assumption is that the external environment—both perceived and real—plays a major role in the organization's success or failure. Environmental pressures, issues, and trends could mean that the organization should literally be offering different products or services, or at the least must adapt to significant environmental changes during the coming three to five to ten years. Each organization's environment is unique consisting of elements such as education, technology, economics, politics, demographics, sociological, legal, cultural values, natural resources and international trends.

Organizations engage in scanning at levels that vary in sophistication and depth. For example, one hospital's "environmental scanning activity" is conducted by a small group. The director of purchasing, one marketing representative and the vice president for operations meet for lunch about once a week to talk about "what's going on out there." This group does not use an analyst's research on economic projections, measures of technological development and change, or data and demographic trends. Instead they use their own "intuitive sense" of what's happening in the environment, plus information culled from colleagues, customers and competitors.

At the other end of the scanning spectrum are the groups who use sophisticated, analytical and data-based methods for plotting various trends and changes in the environment. These reports are developed one or more times a year and are presented as a formal environmental assessment (usually in a formal strategic planning process). Some industry groups publish them as reports for their members.

1.2 Internal Analysis. A second component to defining the present is a review of the "internal" aspects of the organization or department. Just as there is an environmental system composed of characteristics such as economic, political and demographic changes, there are internal systems that define the nature of the organization. Future design takes into account both the external and internal

systems—the essence of the systems approach. In one illustrative
model developed by Kast and Rosenweig, the organization is defined as consisting of five subsystems: (1) goals and values, (2)
technical, (3) structural, (4) psychosocial and (5) managerial (14,
15). Each system has components which must be analyzed as to
their strengths and needs, suggesting points to build on or correct.
As a whole, these subsystems and their interrelationships are the organization to be planned for—the target of the redesign and futures
work.

The design/redesign group systematically examines each of the
subsystems, searching for significant strengths and needs through
five questions. What are the competencies and weaknesses of the
technical system? Of the structural system? Of the psychosocial
system? Of the managerial system? Of the cultural system (goals
and values)? Each participant is asked to identify strengths and core
competencies (16). When participants think of the core work of the
organization—medical care in hospitals, counseling in a mental
health agency, legislative activity in an association—what is done
very well? The analysis strives for as complete a description of the
organization as possible. The term weakness is not used, as there is
often a tendency to assign blame. Instead, needs is the identifying
term further differentiated into "what we need to do that the organization is not now doing", and "what we need to do differently."
The latter often stimulates discussion of redesign and organization
change issues.

1.2   Define & Describe Desired Future

Step Two of the model is the creative design or redesign of the
desired future of the organization (or department). Building on
Ackoff's idealized design process, the step requires participants to
design/redesign their organization in any way they want. According
to Ackoff, futures planning involves clearing psychological barriers.
In his view, "Probably the most important property of an idealized
design [is that] . . . it reveals that the principal obstruction between
us and the future we most desire is ourselves. This obstruction can
be removed by a set of mobilizing ideas; an idealized design can
provide such a set of ideas" (17). In this Step, participants take the
position that the organization does not exist. If it could be designed
(it does not really exist in the case of a new organization) or re-

designed in any way at all, how would the participants create it? The purposes of Step 2—creative design/redesign— are several. By engaging in the design work: (1) participants must begin to think creatively about their organization's purposes, structure, and work process from the starting point without existing barriers; (2) participants focus on what they would change—further surfacing issues for organizational attention and development; and (3) participants often inject innovation into organizational structures and processes that may have been in place for years or decades.

The intention is a "zero-based" redesign concept—an opportunity to start fresh. The process attempts to address the problem that prevailing organization structures and processes are too often taken as starting and fixed points. If the environment is changing radically, can we truly believe that the organization does not need to be redesigned? The process itself requires courage from participants because we are called upon to do something new, to confront a no man's land, to push into a forest where there are no well-worn paths and from which no one has returned to guide us. To live into the future means a leap into the unknown.

An idealized design must be: (1) technologically feasible, (2) operationally viable and (3) capable of rapid learning and adaptation.

> "The product of an idealized design is not an ideal system, because it is capable of being improved and improving itself. Therefore, it is not perfect or utopian system. Rather, it is the most effective ideal seeking system of which its designers can conceive. It is that system with which its designers would currently replace the system planned for if they were free to replace it with any system they wanted." (18)

The properties are requirements that insure that proposed designs for the organization's future are not utopian (divorced from the realities of daily operations including constraints of the marketplace). A first outcome is usually dissatisfaction with continuing as is. This, in turn, creates an impetus to define a more desirable state, the ideal.

Importantly, the idealized design/redesign is not a creative "stand-alone" step. The process advocated is not that a planning group simply begin with a new vision. Beginning with vision-building effort is sterile without data, without sensitivity to the existing external and internal systems. This step is driven by the group's thinking about changes in the external environment and about the strengths and needs in the five internal organizational systems (Step 1 processes). What then are some topics of the redesign?

The group first is asked to redesign the whole organization, creating a generalized vision. For example, how would a bank of the future be different—triple in size with a greater range of products and services—including securities and insurance? The design group is then asked to construct each subsystem focusing on how these become an integrated and *different* whole.

The technical system is redesigned first, as it is the core work of the organization and what most are focused on. This means a redesign of the products and services and the work system, including production, markets and marketing, product services, support services and the distribution network. The "core technical work" changes depending on whether the organization is a manufacturing plant, hospital, educational or governmental institution or a health and welfare agency.

Next, the structure is redesigned, with the redesign group focusing on such issues as degree of formalization, specialization, standardization, centralization, and the personnel configuration. Would the organization be more or less centralized? Is it too formal—are all meetings taped with detailed minutes circulated widely? Are managers forbidden to cross authority lines?

The psychosocial system receives attention next. How would the planning group redesign the organization with respect to behaviors of individuals and groups with regard to motivation, expectations, needs, status and role systems, group dynamics, leadership and power.

The management system follows, with the redesign efforts directed at the planning, organizing, developing, directing/leading and controlling work. The planning group considers, for example, whether management has a development orientation and whether they are flexible in their leadership style.

Finally, the planning group is asked to consider a redesign of the goals, values, and culture of the organization. Is the culture participative and supportive, for example? Are the heroes of the organization recognized, and is there a cultural network that supports the appropriate values—e.g., performance, quality, innovation.

The future change can be linked to existing quality and reengineering efforts. During a recent visit to a state government agency, we reviewed the grantsmanship activities in a design/redesign context. One participant asked how strategic planning fit into the already existing quality improvement initiative. It became clear that this Bureau of Conservation Services could change its resource distribution work by:

- Continuous improvement of the current grants system reducing cycle time, proposed requirements and reporting
- Reengineering, eliminating program grants in favor of whole block grants to communities
- Envisioning a whole new approach, eliminating the need for grants altogether.

1.3 Critical Gap Analysis

In Step Three redesigners conduct a comparative analysis of the present and the future. Analysts look for differences—a gap or gaps —between the current structure and functioning of the organization and the vision of the future. For example, the intention to create a participative, empowered work force (characteristics of the future) is compared to the current management approach (top down, solitary decision making) and lack of a structure of teams and groups for employee input. System by system analysis leads to a set of "gaps" to be addressed during the implementation of the redesign.

1.4 Define Leading Strategies

Strategy has been defined as position, perspective, pattern and plan (19). Here we are using strategy to mean a direction destination and decision guide. For example, some years ago one medical college determined that the school was too small to support teaching, research and clinical activities of the region. A growth strategy was announced with the intention of adding beds, research capability and faculty support. In Step Four, a strategy or set of strategies is selected to represent the "direction—destination—decisions" that are driving the redesign (20). For another example, a bank branch office was identified as redundant following a merger of two large regional banks. In an effort to consolidate buildings and people, the new "super regional bank" saw "closure" as the strategy best representing the direction (leaner), destination (fewer branches) and decisions (transfer of employees and accounts). Strategy is here used as a way to organize *perspective* about the future, to begin to develop a *pattern of behaviors* and decisions and to *position* the redesigned organization for success.

1.5 Identify Resource Requirements

Redesign implies and requires the addition of new resources or the redistribution of existing ones. Each redesign effort must identify the resource requirements in terms of (5.1) production process, (5.2) personnel, (5.3) facility, (5.4) equipment and supplies, and (5.5) finances. To successfully implement the new design, production process needs such as training must be identified as well as staff requirements, space, equipment and an overall budget. The resource requirements sketched out in Step 5.0 are refined in the final step linking the changes to operations work.

1.6 Operational Start: Actions, Responsibilities and Evaluation

This Step 6 links the vision of the desired future, strategies and actions to operations and budgeting. Following the systems model, the planning participants must now consider five topics: objectives; program planning; outcome expectations; responsibility assignments; and budgeting. This Step—linking redesign to operations —establishes the ties between the "designed desired future" and the near-term work of year-to-year operations. Few organizations need to be introduced to this work for the first time.

There are five parts to this linkage process. First, the planning group must create program objectives. Second, the planning group must subject the programs proposed to detailed operations-oriented analyses. Third, the group must define what the year-to-year outcome expectations are and how to know when yearly progress is successful (performance indicators). Fourth, responsibility analyses and then responsibility assignments must be made in order to insure that persons in charge are directly connected to the proposed programs and actions. Fifth, the proposed programs and the whole set of strategies and actions must be connected to the budget—how does the vision of the future and the planning strategies and programs relate to the current and future funding structure?

In working through the steps just listed, the roles of the chief executive and planner are critical. The CEO must co-design the process and act as champion throughout. Working on the future is a crucial part of the chief executive's role. The planner is engaged in both *process* and *content* roles. As the team proceeds through the steps, process roles are: co-designer, catalyst, educator, negotiator, and advocate. The planner designs the planning procedure with the CEO and acts as catalyst up and down the organization, continuously advocating a "futures orientation." The content roles of the planner are: fact finder (collecting and analyzing data on internal and external environments), options analyst and strategy finder (not always, or often, inventor of new strategy). Thus the planner helps to "work the process" and provides substantive input at certain points.

Results to Date

Commentators have criticized strategic planning on many points of purpose, design and impact. Alexander Hiam listed four sources of error which he termed myths (21).

> Myth 1: Standard statements and reports give a clean picture of strategic position.

> Myth 2: The sum of business unit plans is a good plan for the company.

> Myth 3: Good strategic leadership at headquarters translates into good strategies at the business unit level.

> Myth 4: Products are mortal.

So what do these myths mean to Mark our CEO? In his company, the "usually collected data," including the financials, are not rich enough for strategy building. Adding his various divisional vice presidents' plans together neglects the value-added effects of creative synergy. He must create the synergy in collaboration with his executives. And, mortal products thought to be dying can be revived. As Ohmae reminds us, Yamaha certainly demonstrated this last point by adding compact disks to a musical instrument, turning around a fading market for an old well-known product—the piano (22).

What are some other problems with strategic planning? In 1994 Henry Mintzberg listed several for a start saying that strategic planning discourages commitment, is conservative, tends to create political activity and is obsessed with control. A successful redesign of strategic planning must address why executives are not committed, whether the process produces anything revolutionary, how to control politics in the organization and how *not* to try to predict events when we cannot.

Several experts responded to this criticism. John Bryson says:

> To deliver the best results, strategic planning requires broad yet effective information gathering, development and exploration of strategic alternatives, and an emphasis on future implications of present decisions. Strategic planning can help facilitate communication and participation, accommodate divergent interests and values, foster wise and reasonably analytic decision making, and promote successful implementation (23).

Several authors have added new ways to foster participation, new methods of tracking strategies and of monitoring progress . In recent writings, commentators have suggested that strategic success depends on leadership (24); on an understanding of the meaning of strategy (25,26) and on balance and broad actions during execution (27).

So the process seems to hold great potential for private companies and public agencies. Yet many leaders are intimidated and disappointed by mediocre or failed strategic processes. Why?

> A baseball player once told a coach that she wanted to quit "Why" he asked?
> "It just got too hard," she said.
> He thought for only a second and yelled back
> "It's supposed to be hard. If it wasn't hard, everyone would do it—The HARD is what makes it great."
>   Jimmy Dugan to Dottie Henson
>   A League of Their Own

If it is that hard, why don't we just quit talking about strategy? Because strategy leads companies and institutions to *direction, decisions* and *destinations* that determine survival and success. Consider these examples and their importance.

- Decades ago Woolworth Company executives might have popped champaign to celebrate their enduring and successful nationwide strategy of 5&10 cent stores.
- More recently, Disney would consider animation as a focus for company development along with new theme park locations and worldwide distribution of its products in Disney stores.
- Tandy Corporation would set the stage for this advertisement in 1996: "RadioShack-perhaps the ultimate service/convenience store for consumer electronics. There's a RadioShack within five minutes of where almost every American lives or works."
- Penn State University targets "distance education" for strategic attention because using technology to take teaching to the student *is* the future.
- Microsoft at first barely recognizes the Internet, but then moves creatively and aggressively to embrace it.
- *Your local hospital* considers merging with a long standing competitor, upsetting years of tradition and loyalty in the community and among medical staffs.

As a designer, facilitator and participant of many strategic planning processes over nearly thirty years, I believe the problems are driven by errors in assumptions and procedures. It often seems like leaders have neglected the fundamentals—as if they missed their blocks and tackles in football or fumbled the fingering and scales at a concert performance. Learning strategic planning for me means relearning the main principles of strategy formation and planning. The lessons presented here are composites of ones I have observed in actual cases but do not represent any one organization.

The subjects are organized in three general areas:

- Lessons of Purpose, Philosophy and Concept
- Lessons of Design and Methods
- Lessons of Progress, Outcomes and Benefits.

When possible, each of the "lessons" is related to others. With reflection, experienced executives, managers, and board members will see the connection of design, processes and expected outcomes. Following each of the three general parts is a set of cases for use in teaching and learning. The cases cover a wide range of illustrations, public and private organizations, large and small. When I use the cases for graduate seminars I expect students to add material from the companies' and agencies' web sites and I ask the students to address the following questions in their case analyses.

1. What are the strategic issues facing this organization?
2. Who are the stakeholders—customers, suppliers, competitors, regulators…?
3. What are the external environmental threats and opportunities?
4. What are the internal strengths and weaknesses of the organization?
5. What is the stated or implied vision of the future?
6. What are the lead strategies for moving toward the future?
7. What methods would you use to start or improve strategic planning in this type of organization?
8. What additional data would you like to have for planning purposes?

Students and readers will encounter a wide range of plans, organization types, and both explicit and implicit strategies. The diversity of the cases broadens readers' abilities to think strategically across industries and fields.

Summary

This synthesized procedure for design/redesign is a part of the movement toward development of a consensus process. Leaders have recognized the need to redesign their organizational systems but are confronted by a bewildering set of process choices. Many of these alternatives have a common systems thinking core. To take advantage of this commonality, we must have more systems educated leaders with an understanding of the roots of this work (28, 29, 30, 31, 32).

Most recently, commentators on strategy formation and planning have approached the subject by considering alternative images of the formative process and strategy itself (33). They have considered the nature of the process (34, 35) as an activity and as a practical challenge (36) along with the importance of execution (37). We need to extend our thinking about this core process and its desired contribution to meeting future change needs.

Issues of purpose, philosophy and concept begin our learning.

Notes
[1] Anderson, O.W. *The Health Services Continuum in Democratic States.* Ann Arbor, MI: Health Administration Press, 1989.
[2] Ackoff, R.L. *A Concept of Corporate Planning.* New York: Wiley, 1970.
[3] Ackoff, R.L. *Creating the Corporate Future: Plan or Be Planned For.* New York: Wiley, 1981.
[4] Vancil, R.F. "Strategy Formulation in Complex Organizations" In: P. Lorange and R.F. Vancil, *Strategic Planning Systems* Englewood Cliffs, New Jersey, 1977, p.4.
[5] Deming, W.E. *Out of Crisis.* Cambridge, MA: MIT Press, 1986.
[6] Juran, J.M. *Juran on Planning for Quality.* New York: Free Press, 1988.
[7] Crosby, P. *Quality is Free.* New York: McGraw-Hill, 1979
[8] Hammer, M. "Reengineering Work: Don't Automate, Obliterate." *Harvard Business Review.* Vol. 90, no. 4 (July-Aug 1990), 104-112.
[9] Hyde, A.C. "A Primer on Process Reengineering." *The Public Manager.* Vol. 24, no. 21 (Spring 1995), 55-68.
[10] Ackoff, R.L. *A Concept of Corporate Planning.* Op. cit. note 2.
[11] Ackoff, R.L. *Creating the Corporate Future.* Op. cit. note 3.
[12] Ackoff, R.L. "The Circular Organization Design: An Update." *Academy of Management Executive.* 3; 1989, 11-16.
[13] Mintzberg, H. "The Fall and Rise of Strategic Planning" *Harvard Business Review.* Jan-Feb 1994, 107-114.
[14] Kast, F.E.; Rosenzweig, J.E. *Organization and Management.* New York: McGraw Hill, 1985.
[15] Ziegenfuss, J. T. *Designing Organizational Futures.* Springfield, Illinois.: Charles C. Thomas 1985.
[16] Prahalad, C.K.; Hamel, G. "The Core Competencies of the Corporation." *Harvard Business Review.* May-June 1990, 79-91.
[17] Ackoff, R.L. *Creating the Corporate Future.* Op. Cit. see note 3, p. 123.
[18] Ibid, 1981, p. 107.
[19] Mintzberg, H. *The Rise and Fall of Strategic Planning: Reconceiving Roles for Planning, Plans, Planners.* New York: Free Press, 1994.
[20] Ziegenfuss, J.T. *Relearning Strategic Planning: Lessons of Philosophy & Procedure.* Lawrence, Kansas: Allen Press, 1996.
[21] Hiam, A. "Exposing Four Myths of Strategic Planning" *Journal of Business Strategy.* Sept/Oct 1990; 23-28.
[22] Ohmae, K. "Getting Back to Strategy" *Harv. Business Rev.* Nov-Dec, 1988.
[23] Bryson, J.M. *Strategic Planning for Public and Non-Profit Organizations.* San Francisco, CA: Jossey Bass, 1995.
[24] Ireland, R.D.; Hitt, M.A. "Achieving and maintaining strategic competitiveness in the 21st century: the role of strategic leadership." *Acad. Mgmt Executive* 19(4); 2005, pp 63-78.
[25] Hambrick, D.C.; Fredrickson, J.W. "Are you sure you have a strategy?" *Acad Mgmt Executive* 19(4); 2005; pp 51-62.
[26] Gavetti, G.; Ryan, J.W. "How strategists really think." *Harvard Business Review.* 83(4); 2005; p. 54.
[27] Kaplan, R.S.; Norton, D.P. "Building a strategy Focused Organization" *Harvard Business Review.* 1999.

[28] Ziegenfuss, J.T. "Are You Growing Systems Thinking Managers? Use a Systems Model to Teach and Practice Organizational Analysis and Planning, Policy and Development." *Systems Practice.* 5(5); 1992; 509-527.

[29] Ziegenfuss, J.T. *The Organizational Path to Health Care Quality.* Ann Arbor, MI: Health Administration Press, 1993.

[30] Ziegenfuss, J.T. "Toward a General Procedure for Quality Improvement: The Double Track Process." *American Journal of Medical Quality.* 9(2):90-97 (1994).

[31] Ziegenfuss, J.T. *Organization and Management Problem Solving: A Systems & Consulting Approach.* Thousand Oaks, Ca. Sage 2002.

[32] Ziegenfuss, J.T. "SystemsThinking Engineers Solve Productivity Problem." *Environmental Engineer.* 41(4) December 2005.

[33] Cummings, S. ; Wilson, D. (Eds). *Images of Strategy.* Oxford: Blackwell, 2003.

[34] Ackerman, F.; Eden, C. *The Practice of Making Strategy: A Step by Step Guide.* Thousand Oaks, Calif. Sage 2005.

[35] Gruenig, R.; Kuehn, R. *Process Based Strategic Plans.* Frankfurt: Springer Verlag, 2005.

[36] Allison, M. Kaye, J. *Strategic Planning for Nonprofit Organizations: A Practical Guide and Workbook.* Hoboken, N.J. : Wiley, 2005.

[37] Hrebiniak, L.G. *Making Strategy Work: Leading Effective Execution and Change.* Upper Saddle River, N.J. Wharton School Pub., 2005.

Part 1

LESSONS OF PURPOSE & PHILOSOPHY & CONCEPT

Many board members, executives and managers must relearn the fundamentals—including better understanding of the philosophy and concepts of planning and strategy formation. In this first section are lessons related to the purpose of planning in the public and private organization.

Boards sometimes do not understand their role while in other cases they tend to be so much involved that they neglect to account for the opinions and ideas of managers and employees. Some leaders feel that any planning system will do—ignoring completely the concept of fitting the planning system with the organizational culture. Thus, executives try to implement a *formal* planning system in what has traditionally been a very *informal* organization—leading to disaster.

In still other organizations planning means paying attention only to additions of new products and services. Executives and boards are quite willing to delay or avoid deletions. These gaps in understanding of purpose, philosophy and concept co-produce problems in planning. This first part offers lessons on the following subjects.

- purpose, importance and definition
- leadership, involvement and roles
- philosophy including relation to the past, to systems thinking and to culture
- assumptions regarding expected change, goals, constraints and risk.

FUTURE SHOCK

Lesson 1: Board executives and employees did not create their own vision of the future, and were surprised by the future created for them.

What happens to a large organization confronted with a major international competitor? What becomes of the small private company that relies on one major buyer of its products? Will the privately practicing professional—physician, lawyer, accountant—with one major client continue to be successful?

Cases of neglect of a changing environment—in which long standing clients or customers switch to competitors—can lead to future shock; the end of a business, a small company or a private practice. Sometimes the company does not die but "merely" experiences a series of severe financial and organizational struggles. For example, Motorola has relied on Apple as a buyer of its chips.

Continued success depends on a purposeful plan for the future that accounts for customers, competitors and environment. Some years ago we discussed with great interest a book by Alvin Toffler entitled Future Shock. We have the concept but we can relearn the planning point.

THE SHOCK OF A FUTURE NOT DESIRED IS SHOCK GENERATED BY LACK OF ATTENTION TO CREATING THE FUTURE WE DO DESIRE.

It is unlikely that we will be shocked by a future that we planned for.

Illustration. The owner of Tranship—a shipping and distribution company with only a few employees and two trucks—built his business by serving a major private company in one local geographic area for 12 years. Because of the pressures of increasing competition at both the national and international levels, the large company decided to relocate. Since it was impossible for Tranship to relocate along with the large buyer of its services, the company was forced to search for other customers under conditions of severe financial uncertainty. At no point had Tranship attempted to create its future—proactively moving to expand its customer base. Over 12 years the company focused only on its major buyer and thus was shocked by the future it found itself in.

DOORS TO THE FUTURE

Lesson 2: Board members, executives, managers and employees opened the wrong door to the future.

"Doors to the future" lead to different implementation paths. A large private company, a public governmental agency, a small private professional practice, a corner grocery store, or a university department are all organizations with choices. Many planning efforts neglect to focus our attention on the choices—alternative doors with different outcomes.

Think of three options. Door 1 is the future defined by the past. This future requires very little creativity from the planners as it presents a mirror image of the past. This future is hoped to hold success despite the fact that the present is changing rapidly and that the environment of the future is unlikely to be the same.

Door 2 leads to a future defined by regulators and competitors. When board members, executives, managers and employees choose this door, they choose to allow their future to be defined by others. In America there is increasingly more awareness that competitors, regulators and foreign companies and countries will not be reticent to define your future for you, a vision that may be exceedingly undesirable.

Door 3 leads to a path created by the organization's leaders. In public and private companies board members, executives, managers and employees are encouraged to assertively define their organization's future. Given an opportunity to create *their* vision, leaders define their company or agency's future products and services, their organizational structure, the desired quality of their work life, their management style and the core values that define their corporate culture. They create the future they *want* to be in.

Illustration. One professional group in particular—physicians—have tended to be reactive about their future. In the last ten years, corporations, consumers, and governmental agencies have become increasingly concerned about medical care costs and about the role of the physician in the health and medical care system. There have been a flurry of health care reform proposals and changes in medical reimbursement that will over time define the physician's future. Physicians have reacted very strongly on the local, state and national level. But on the whole they have done very little in the way of opening Door 3—designing their own future. Their reactions have been characterized by the opening of Door 2, allowing their future to be created by competitors and regulators.

Following a different path through Door 3 requires ideas and proposals for the future of health care reform, for practice models and for academic medicine, not just a response to the ideas and presentations of others. Increasingly in medical schools and in state societies, physicians have begun to open Door 3—defining for the first time the future they would most like to be in.

LEADERSHIP

Lesson 3: The planners and strategists were young staff—bright eyed and bushy tailed—but not the organization's leaders.

The choice of who is to engage in planning and strategy formation is critical. Sometimes there is a tendency to select mostly new employees—often young people with different ideas, excitement and enthusiasm and limited connections to tradition. However, newer employees, managers, executives may not have the power and authority needed to push the plan into action, nor will they have a sense of the richness of the past.

Without the organization's true senior leaders—those recognized formally by position and informally by respect and expertise—the shortfall of personal authority and power undercuts strategic action.

Illustration. In 520 bed Walnut Community Hospital, the transition in leadership was the initiative for a strategic review. Walnut Hospital had long been recognized as a valuable provider of quality clinical care to the community. Over its financially successful history, the board of directors was chaired by a local businessman with charismatic power and highly developed organizational and managerial skills. The chairman and board members were experienced planners in their own companies.

However, for the strategic review, the board "delegated" the planning process to a group of senior hospital executives that did not include board members. This did not appear to be a problem at the outset since the board planned to take the group's recommendations in whole and implement them. But as the planning progressed, it was clear that the board had an unstated vision of Walnut Hospital's future that did not match the executive group's vision. The executive group had the skills and abilities to plan. But the concept of creating a vision as a cooperative, collaborative initiative by both board members and executives was missing. Using only board *or* staff leads to a vision of the future representative of only a part of the leadership.

IMPORTANCE RECOGNIZED

Lesson 4: The leaders felt that planning was essential—but they didn't tell anyone.

In some organizations the creative process and the vision of the organization's future is its best kept secret. While confidentiality protects strategic advantage, it is crucial that board members, executives, managers and employees know that a vision of the future is important, is required and that it is under development. The mere act of *telling* employees and managers signals that considering future purposes and activities are important. Quite obviously the opposite is also true—a future unmentioned is a future dismissed.

When a future is planned by a few key board members and executives, the hard decisions become suspect and the extra effort required is never made. Managers and employees are unlikely to put their shoulders to someone else's wheel. Lower level management and employees may not agree with the vision created by others. In large complex organizations the subverting of the best laid plans of senior leaders is often developed to a high art form (and is viewed as obstructionist). This behavior is actually a rational protest born of being left out of the design work. Keeping visionary thinking secret is a hazard.

Illustration. At North State University the president initiated a university-wide strategic planning process. Not only did the president feel that the process would assist the university, but he felt that he should be personally involved and that he should begin with a letter to the whole academic community. As the planning got underway this president continued to "tell" the academic community that the planning process was important by paying attention to the ideas and designs presented and by being visible in the process.

In contrast to this very public "telling" of the planning process, a dean in one small specialty college elected to create the future in private with minimal involvement of department level faculty, with no involvement of students and with no communication about the process. The dean did in fact create a vision of his college's future, but the importance of the process, the importance of the future and the successful implementation of the plan were undercut by his inability to have the vision recognized by the whole academic community.

FOCUS ON THE PAST

Lesson 5: By only discussing what we've always done, we've neglected to consider what we should be doing.

Are we retaining and supporting the best of the past or are we *clinging* to it? We must relearn how to use the past in planning. Organizations with a rich tradition of success should not be quick to pitch their history in the quest for new adventures, be they products or services. Building on the long tested core competency is key. But retaining an interest in the past despite pressures for change and a new environment is an attempt to maintain an old formula. Russell Ackoff defines quite clearly this focus on the past.

> The reactive planner walks into the future facing the past. He has a
> good view of where the organization has been and is, but no view
> of where it is going. Such planning is like trying to drive a train
> from its caboose.

This lesson, that an interest in all aspects of the organization's life cycle—past, present and future—is critical.

Illustration. There are two illustrations relevant here—one a private company, the other a professional practice. The first case concerns a construction company with a focus on one aspect of the transportation system. Qualityconstruct primarily worked on the building and maintenance of highways. Many transportation system designers recognize that highways cannot continue to be constructed at the same rate as they have been in the past. Already our cities are overrun by expressways and parking lots. However, with the highway construction company's focus on its tradition of highway building, it was unable to think about the future in different ways. The task for Qualityconstruct—and the challenge—was how to build on its rich history of highway construction, creating a broader perspective that includes alternatives such as bullet trains and air transportation support.

A second illustration involves a group of tradition—bound attorneys. Their focus on their strong corporate law achievements of the past put them at a distinct disadvantage as they began to think about services to their clients in the future. Although Smith, Smith & Young had a very strong corporate client group, they did not understand the degree to which major corporations are paying increasing attention to legal expenses. With its history of high revenue work in this area, the firm was clinging to the past even though the clients and the services they request may not be the same in the future.

Note
Ackoff, R.L. "Participation Within Organizations." Wharton Alumni Magazine. Summer 1985.

MANDATES & CONSTRAINTS

Lesson 6: As loyal employees of the state government agency, we accepted the mandates and constraints, then lowered our vision, and eliminated our motivation.

Some commentators on strategic planning suggest that any planning process should begin by defining the mandates and constraints that will affect the organization, either public agency or private company. In their view, only by beginning with the mandates and constraints can you begin to bound what the organization can do. The mandates and constraints define the limits of the organization's activities. This is, however, an error.

The acceptance of mandates and constraints as one of the philosophical points—and often a starting point of the planning process—is extremely detrimental to motivation and creativity. Russell Ackoff has said this best: "The largest obstruction between us and the future we most desire is ourselves." We bring to the process too many obstructions. Adding all the constraints of interested outsiders builds a tight box indeed.

When the planning team begins its work by accepting boundaries on the organization's potential breadth of mission and concept of the future, an inhibiting process flows through the planning group. Planning begins to focus on a narrowness inherent in a future that is already predefined. By accepting what outside stakeholders provide as the boundaries of the organization, executives, managers and employees never get to "push the envelope." The true breakthroughs in organizational development and entrepreneurial success come from a refusal to accept the mandates and constraints of the existing system.

Illustration. As an example we can consider the case of a state Department of Transportation (DOT). The mandates and constraints spell out quite clearly what this organization is to do. But the mandates have little to do with the emphasis of the department (in the future), nor do they say much about traditional versus new technologies. Mandates and constraints define the boundaries in global terms, often historical in nature.

As one strategic direction, the DOT could use most of its time and resources to address public transportation systems in cities. Directed at the poor and the elderly, this direction would make the transportation department a supporter of certain citizen groups over others, e.g. toward the poor and away from business and toward the city rather than suburban and rural communities.

And with some creativity the DOT could reach to support innovative transportation systems, e.g., bullet trains. This embrace of new technologies might be regarded as outside existing boundaries (the mandates and constraints). But it is *within* the purview of an exciting vision of a transportation agency's future. Creativity in strategic futures is all about breaking constraints, not accepting them.

INCREMENTAL VS. STRATEGIC CHANGE

Lesson 7: Continuous, incremental change reduces the number of wrenching upheavals that occur—sometimes below the number needed.

Some planning systems seem designed to move the organization incrementally into the future—one slight adjustment at a time. Other organizations look for bold new strokes—creative products or services or structure—that put the organization into a new future by way of a major strategic leap. There is, in fact, no one best way. IBM and companies in similar situations sometimes need revolution not evolution.

The question here, where is your organization in its life cycle and what level of change is needed? Hayes has summed up nicely the American orientation to strategic leaping:

> One approach ... is through a series of strategic leaps, a few giant upward steps at critical moments. These leaps may take a variety of forms: a product redesign, a large-scale factory modernization or expansion, a move to another location that promises great improvement in wage rates or labor relations, an acquisition of a supplier of a critical material or component, or adoption of a new manufacturing technology. Between taking these giant steps, managers seek only incidental improvements in competitiveness, as the company digests the last step and contemplates the next.   .

In the 1980s we laughed at the prospect of a fourth television network. CBS, NBC and ABC were well entrenched and most thought them to be permanently unbeatable. Fox Broadcasting Company was thought of as a young "also ran" eventually to be defeated. But Fox, with a strong emerging line of shows, had a "strategic leap" in mind. The company bid for and won the rights to broadcast the football games of the National Football League—rights long held by CBS. Credibility and long term potential were immediate payoffs of the strategic leap onto a new level playing field with major rivals.

Other companies take a different path, as Hayes notes.

> At the opposite extreme ... a company may try to progress through a series of small steps whose cumulative impact will be just as great. Rather than rely on a series of discontinuities, such a company continuously strives to bolster its competitive position through a variety of incremental improvements.

To continue to grow incrementally when the competition is nibbling away at your product or service base is an error. Steel companies facing foreign competition and hospitals competing with managed care companies are examples. Over just a few years the organization will vanish because incremental changes are necessary but not sufficient. Conversely, searching for the strategic leap at every turn ignores two problems. First, regular strategic leaps are literally not possible as creativity cannot be planned that tightly. And second, even strategically leaping organizations need incremental development to support their gains.

Illustration. The Robeers Campus of Southern University was making nice progress over its twenty some year history. But this progress was mostly incremental in nature. Senior faculty of the organization and board members realized that in order for the campus to progress, a series of strategic leaps was necessary. Instead of proposing the kind of growth that had occurred in the past—the addition of three to eight percent per year growth in students and one or two new programs and several faculty—planners with fast growth in mind suggested major changes. For example, the addition of a new $15 million library, the conversion of the senior and graduate program campus to a four year college, the merger with a local community college, and the acquisition of a nearby industrial plant's facilities with one hundred acres of grounds were listed. Taking these steps, the Robeers Campus would strategically leap into quite a different future than its incremental past would imply.

Notes
Hayes, R.H. "Strategic Planning Forward in Reverse?" *Harvard Business Review.* Nov-Dec 1985; p. 114.

TO CREATE OR CONTROL

Lesson 8: Planning is both following the flock and leading the flock astray (from usual practices).

The strategic planning literature summarizes the planning process as either "creativity inducing" or "controlling." The paradox is that we want it to be both. Many leaders begin the process with the sense that new products and services are needed. Or that there are new markets to be tapped. The planning effort focuses on discovering ideas that "break the mold" or that represent "thinking outside the box" (two well known clichés). By definition, creativity is a resistance of the status quo, an effort to devise a new path. Simultaneously, large complex organizations require that many units and persons pursue a coordinated path—control is needed.

Illustration. Some years ago, Southeastern State University, a large public land grant institution, came to see its graduate programs as lagging behind comparable institutions. Administrative leaders proposed a significant new push into graduate education and research. Long standing faculty were devoted to undergraduates and had built a solid national reputation for undergraduate education. While faculty saw graduate education and research as a threat (leading them away from their cherished and traditional undergraduate focus), administrators saw this new strategy as a means to build institutional strength and expanded national presence. For administrators, this was an opportunity to pursue while protecting undergraduate strength.

GOALS NOT CHOSEN

Lesson 9: We never decided *not* to do anything.

Well run planning sessions generate excitement about opportunities—for new programs, for new services, for new products. Quite often the number of new ideas is pleasantly surprising. However, considerably less exhilarating is the notion that the new ideas can only come to fruition if some existing activities end. Someone must agree to kill their program, service or product. This means that the group as a whole must consider which products, programs, and services will not be pursued.

The giving up of goals is one of the most difficult parts of the strategy planning process, the part which many organizations fail. A simple test of the effectiveness of your planning process is to ask which goals, products, services and programs were *not* chosen during this iteration of planning.

Illustration. Program areas were defined as the organizing elements for the planning process at United Social Services, a small non-profit organization with eight staff and twenty-five board members. The program areas (eight in all) included education and training, transportation, counseling, marketing, public information, administration, and legislative activities. The planning group analyzed and discussed the eight areas with enthusiasm. By the conclusion of the assessment and objective setting for each of the areas, they had added two or three new products or services to each area. For example, a new survey of client satisfaction was added to marketing, several new workshops and locations in education, and a new administrative information system for management.

Although the planning consultant was not particularly attentive to the demeanor of the staff at the beginning, she noticed that as the group progressed through the areas the staff became almost despondent about the additions. It was not until the end of the process that the consultant understood that the board and staff in an excited collaboration, had added thirty percent to the workload for the coming year but no new resources. At the conclusion of their "planning process" they had decided not to drop anything.

For this group, planning was defined as the addition of new products and services within existing resource levels (including financial base and staff support). Managing this problem requires that the group answer the hard question "what do we choose not to do next year?"

UNCERTAINTY

Lesson 10: Until the uncertainty was eliminated, the group refused to act.

Some executives, board members, managers and employees think that planning is a controlled, rational process by which uncertainty about the company's future is removed. To the contrary, when new ideas, products or services are proposed, the number of unknown outcomes often rises. Hrebiniak and Joyce call the process we use "intended rationality":

> Our contention is that managers intend to be rational when formulating and implementing strategy, but that rationality is bounded by limited cognitive and information processing capacities. Within limitations, the intention of managers is to (1) focus on utilitarian outcomes in strategic planning, (2) design organizations to mini-

mize costs of coordination and optimize efficiency and effectiveness, and (3) develop incentives and controls that motivate and
reinforce acceptable performance.

Planning does *not* remove uncertainty but it does limit the degree
of surprise that the organization must handle. Thus, planning is uncertainty management. When board members, executives, managers
and employees refuse to act until uncertainty is eliminated—until
we have compulsively planned every last detail—the organization is
frozen in time. Unfortunately, by waiting until all details are defined
those managed first have now changed again.

Illustration. The Traffic Safety Society is a small non-profit
organization that lobbies for regulation to support highway safety.
Successful over a period of years, the state in which they operated
duly created the legislation they proposed and implemented their
plan to protect young children with seat restraints.

However, their funding was provided by a combination of state,
federal and private sources. With the completion of their mission,
they could expect that the purpose for their organization would
change. More so than most, the Traffic Safety Society was forced to
confront the problem with managing the uncertainty of a very different future. Their old mission accomplished, what was to be their
new mission?

Here is uncertainty of the highest level. Old programs, services,
finances and staff might be unavailable, less useful or both in their
new future. Few organizations confront that absolute level of uncertainty, but managing and adapting to the uncertainties of a changing
environment is a part of the natural process for all organizations.

Notes
Hrebiniak, L.G.; Joyce, W.F. Implementing Strategy. 1984; New York: MacMillan, p. 7.

EXCITEMENT

Lesson 11: The strategy planning process was viewed as one long
committee meeting with no agenda and no end in sight.

Excitement must be a characteristic of the planning experience.
Without it new ideas are few, resulting in planners who respond to

the future by repeating the past. Meetings are dull and boring, so it is easier to reiterate in non-think fashion the programs, activities and agenda of the organization's history.

There are common signs of this problem. Members of the planning committee show up late, or do not show up at all. Conversation often turns from the topics at hand to sports, social activities, or organizational politics. Members frequently ask at what time the meetings will end and avoid rescheduling follow-up meetings at any early date. Ms. Fry a college administrator was quite descriptive.

> This morning, I reluctantly went to a planning meeting scheduled to last three hours. It did. I almost didn't. I survived it, only to have the convener announce that we had accomplished so much and had generated so many good ideas, we must meet again next week for three hours! I got out of the room fast to avoid being rude.

In one departmental meeting of research scientists at the start of a multi-year planning process, an initial call for ideas generated very few responses from the group. Participants knew from past experience that no actions were taken on their ideas. At that time, the planning process was fairly new with participants unsure about expectations—excitement was low. Planning appeared to be a forced undertaking by the top executives.

In contrast, when members feel that the design of the future is collaborative and encouraging of new ideas they want to be a part. They show up early, they work late and they talk enthusiastically about possibilities.

Senior scientists in the department above gradually found that their views were sincerely desired. The planning process was opened up by a series of participative retreats so that by the end of the third year, scientists were submitting pages of ideas and suggestions for programs and services, much beyond the required minimum.

Some executives have different strategies for generating both new ideas and excitement. Wolf Schmitt at Rubbermaid uses novel techniques, some of which make it to the formal strategy process according to Martin.

> Let me tell you how the CEO of America's most admired corporation gets new product ideas:
>
> He communes with trees and plants.
> He listens to children, including his own.

He sends his creative people to Chinese restaurants. In China.
He depends heavily on intuition, not much on analysis.
He watches trends—but not just positive trends. He draws
many ideas from unfavorable trends.

Above all, Wolfgang Schmitt is thinking, always thinking. When
he scouts a museum in San Francisco or looks into a competitor's
show window in Milan, he wonders, Is there an idea here that we
can use to create a new product or improve an old design?

Illustration. Perhaps the best example of this problem occurred
at the conclusion of a relatively brief strategic planning process.
The American Bank's board of directors agreed to meet in three,
three-hour sessions over a two-week period to create a first draft of
their vision of the future. The first two sessions were pretty much
a struggle. It was entirely unclear whether or not the organization
was truly committed to creating something very new. Some directors wanted to sell American Bank, others wanted to merge, a few
even suggested acquisitions. But most were content. The lack of
excitement was disguised, to be polite.

Not until the executive's presentation of his vision of the future
toward the end of the third meeting did the situation become clear.
At the conclusion the president called for questions. There was a
somewhat awkward pause.

One director said, "Before we get into that, is there anymore
coffee?"

Further explanations were unnecessary. If you need coffee to
stay awake to discuss the company's vision, excitement is absent.

CASES

CASE 1: ANESTHESIA DEPARTMENT—ACADEMIC MEDICAL CENTER

The health and medical care industry has recently been confronting
the need to change. Hospitals, insurance companies and physician
groups have been thinking about new directions and delivery system
alternatives. This report on strategic planning in an academic medical department illustrates how one group of physicians attempted to

become proactive. The case describes the philosophy and purposes of strategic planning, the need to connect Department level planning to the greater system, procedural steps, and the actions taken and benefits received in the early reviews. The case demonstrates one model for strategic planning across fields and industries.

See: Biebuyck, J.F.; Ziegenfuss, J.T. "How Physicians Can Create Their Future." *Physician Executive.* Volume 18 Number 4; July-August, 1992, pp. 31-36

Questions: Would this model work as a guide for strategic planning with other physicians' organizations, and with other organizations outside the medical field?

CASE 2: AMTRAK

Commercial and recreational transportation is a vital part of our society. The well-known name "Amtrak" is the blending of the words "American" and "track." The railroad's official name is the National Railroad Passenger Corporation. It first began on May 1, 1971, when Clocker No. 235 departed New York Penn Station at 12:05 a.m. bound for Philadelphia. In 1971, Amtrak announced a schedule of 184 trains, serving 314 destinations. Since the beginning, even-numbered trains have traveled north and east. Odd-numbered trains travel south and west.

Today Amtrak serves more than 500 stations in 46 states, employing approximately 19,700 people. Every day, approximately 68,000 passengers travel on 300 trains, excluding commuter trains that Amtrak operates under contract. Operating over more than 22,000 route miles, it owns 650 of the route miles, primarily between Boston and Washington, DC, and in Michigan. In other parts of the country, Amtrak trains use tracks owned by freight railroads. Amtrak uses alliances with different companies to offer its customers every kind of facility from rental car to hotels to Greyhound buses. American Automobile Association members receive a 10% discount. Alaska Airlines mileage plan members receive mileage credit while traveling on Amtrak's Pacific Coast routes.

This year, Amtrak is putting into action an aggressive five-year investment plan to improve the reliability and comfort of trains, facilities and tracks. They want Amtrak passengers to experience improvements in comfort and quality (through greater travel time reductions). Also, to achieve better system efficiency and lower costs, Amtrak is streamlining and downsizing their management structure.

Website: http://www.amtrak.com/

Questions: What are the strategic questions facing Amtrak and what should be its vision of the future?

CASE 3: HENRY FORD HOSPITAL

Today, acute medical care is provided in most communities in the United States. Henry Ford Hospital, founded in October 1915, started with a private patient building. Several other small buildings housed the surgical pavilion, research quarters, kitchens, laundry facilities, the power plant, and garage. The hospital was financed and built by Henry Ford, who organized a closed staff of physicians and surgeons.

Today the hospital has more than 800 physicians, 40 specialties, and 22 Henry Ford Medical Centers. Michigan's managed care plan allows the Henry Ford Health System to handle 2.5 million patient visits annually. With 12,600 employees, Henry Ford Health System is the 6th largest employer in the state. A 45-member board governs the system. Advisory and affiliate boards comprised of 220 trustees provide vital links to the communities served by the system.

The Henry Ford system also includes an educational and research center. The Henry Ford Health Sciences Center is staffed with a full-time academic faculty of 800 physicians and scientists from the Henry Ford Medical Group. The center is a national research leader with programs in several Centers of Excellence, including Henry Ford Bone & Joint Center, Josephine Ford Cancer Center, Henry Ford Heart & Vascular Institute, and the Henry Ford Neuroscience Institute. A broad range of research is conducted in clinical epidemiology, economics, computer science, finance, health education, psychology, sociology and medicine. Most of the funding comes from the National Institutes of Health, Department of Defense, Agency for Health Care Research and Quality, Centers for

Disease Control, and Blue Cross Blue Shield of Michigan's Health-care Research Foundation.

Website: http://www.henryfordhealth.org/

Questions: What are the strategic issues facing the Henry Ford Health System and what is its vision of the future?

CASE 4: MARRIOTT

Every day, many people utilize the services of the hospitality industry during their travels to new foreign and domestic locations. Marriott Hotels' heritage can be traced back to a root beer stand opened in Washington DC, in 1927 by J. Willard and Alice S. Marriott. Today, Marriott International has more than 2,800 lodging properties located in the United States and 69 other countries and territories. It operates franchise hotels under the brands Renaissance Hotels and Resorts, Courtyard, Residence Inn, Fairfield Inn, Towne place suites, Springhill Suites, Ritz-Carlton Hotel and Club and others.

Marriott is the first worldwide hospitality company to have established a formal supplier diversity program, normally contracting or purchasing services like cleaning and maintenance services (e.g., carpet cleaning, windows, janitorial, hood cleaning, etc), dry cleaning, energy and electrical supplies and service, florists, food and beverages, golf and related products, interior design services, IT services, landscaping, marketing and advertising, and waste removal.

Recently Marriott announced the sale of Ramada International hotels. It also completed a transaction with Whitbread, a leading chain of hotels, restaurants, and health and fitness clubs in UK. Marriott now holds a 50/50 joint venture to acquire Whitbread's portfolio of 46 franchised Marriott and Renaissance hotels (more than 8,000 rooms). As part of the joint venture agreement, Marriott assumed management of the hotels, and intends to sell them to new owners subject to long-term Marriott management agreements.

Website: https://marriott.com/default.mi
Questions: What are the strategic issues facing the Marriott Company and how will it continue to develop?

CASE 5: FEMA

Responding to emergencies and managing the wide diversity of contributions from citizens and companies is a great challenge. Recently the Federal Emergency Management Agency was exposed as inefficient and ineffective. FEMA, in responding to Hurricane Katrina, was generally thought to have abandoned tens of thousands of people of New Orleans before and after the hurricane. Before the storm, the authorities issued a mandatory evacuation, but the emergency plans did not address the poor and invalid population, who needed evacuation help. Evacuees ran short of gasoline, food and water. Exits were blocked due to heavy traffic. Following the hurricane, New Orleans was flooded with water, in which floated dead human beings and animals. No water, food or hygiene was available for the surviving population and crime spiraled out of control. Rescue helicopters, ground transportation, and emergency service professionals did not arrive in New Orleans until hours after the disaster. Poor coordination among federal, state and local officials was blamed. There was a total breakdown of communication systems in New Orleans, much like the 9/11 terrorism attack in New York. Many citizens thought faster responses and better planning among FEMA, local government and other federal administration agencies could have avoided this scenario. FEMA is a special target for redesign.

Website:
FEMA: http://www.fema.gov/ .

Questions: Given FEMA's perceived and real failure to manage the New Orleans disaster, what should be the agency's future strategy and direction?

CASE 6: DICKINSON SCHOOL OF LAW—PENN STATE UNIVERSITY

Lawyers are ever present in modern American society. In 2000, Penn State University acquired the previously independent Dickinson School of Law in a new partnership designed to benefit both schools. Dickinson, founded by John Reed in 1834, is the oldest law school in Pennsylvania and fifth oldest in the nation, with a history of graduating quality attorneys. Pennsylvania State University, founded in 1855, is one of the top tier public research universities. It offers post-graduate programs in medicine, engineering, business and (with Dickinson) law.

Dickinson was struggling with outmoded facilities and declining applications, as well as the absence of new technology. This merger enabled Penn State to offer the law degree without starting from zero, while Dickinson gained access to the vast library collection and information technology resources of a major public university.

In 2004, Penn State announced investment of over $100 million in a new dual-campus law school. Along with the existing law school campus in Carlisle, a new campus was to be established at University Park (about 80 miles away). The recently formed law school at University Park has recruited several internationally prominent professors, the diversity of the student body has nearly tripled, the number of applicants for admission has increased by over 50 percent, and the average academic credentials of admitted students have improved significantly. The Penn State Dickinson School of Law now ranks among the nations' top 100 law schools with its dispute resolution program ranking seventh.

Websites: Penn State University: www.psu.edu
Dickinson School of Law: http://www.dsl.psu.edu/

Questions: Will a second campus at University Park add value to the quality of legal education at Penn State? Was this a good strategic move for both Dickinson and Penn State?

CASE 7: PARIS

Strategic planning is needed for large cities as well as organizations. This early report on Paris, France was one of the first efforts to use a systems- oriented approach to strategic planning in a city context. The diversity of changes and pressures confronting Paris meant planners faced a set of interlocking problems—described here as "problematique." The case illustrates the use of systems theory, derived strategy formation processes and the linkages and implications for countrywide changes and national policy.

See Ozbekhan, H. "The Future of Paris: A Systems Study in Strategic Urban Planning." *Philosophical Transactions of the Royal Society of London.* A. 287; 1977, pp.523-544

Web site: www.paris.org/

Questions: What makes strategic planning especially challenging for city planners and for state and national leaders?

CASE 8: NASA

Space and exploration are part of the American cultural heritage. President Dwight D. Eisenhower established the National Aeronautics and Space Administration in 1958, partially in response to the Soviet Union's launch of the first artificial satellite. President John F. Kennedy focused NASA and the nation on sending astronauts to the moon. Through the Mercury and Gemini projects, NASA developed the technology and skills it needed for the journey. On July 20, 1969, Neil Armstrong and Buzz Aldrin became the first of 12 men to walk on the moon, meeting Kennedy's challenge.

NASA headquarters, in Washington, provides overall guidance and direction to the Agency. Ten field centers and a variety of installations conduct the day-to-day work, in laboratories, on airfields, in wind tunnels and in control rooms. NASA conducts its work in four principle organizations, called mission directorates: aeronautics, systems, science, and space operations

This year NASA is planning to reach further across the universe. The Mars Exploration Rovers are still traveling across Mars after more than a year. Cassini is in orbit around Saturn. The Hubble Space Telescope continues to explore the universe. The latest crew of the international space station is extending the permanent human presence in space. Earth Science satellites are sending back unprecedented data on Earth's oceans, climate and other features.

NASA's aeronautics team is working with other government organizations, universities, and industry to fundamentally improve the air transportation experience and retain U.S. leadership in global aviation. NASA has begun returning the space shuttle to flight. The crew of Discovery tested new in-flight safety procedures and carried supplies to the international space station. New priority projects include improving space shuttle safety, continuing work on the international space station, returning to the moon, and building a base for launching human missions beyond the moon, beginning with Mars. Though nearly 50 years old, NASA is beginning an exciting part of its existence.

See Levy, D.H. "What should be NASA'S new direction?" *Parade*. June 13, 2004.

Website: http://www.nasa.com/
Questions: What is NASA's vision of its strategic future?

CASE 9: OLIVE GARDEN

Many of us dine out—some of us regularly, some for special occasions—and experience the full range of restaurant services. General Mills Restaurants, a division of General Mills, Inc, originally developed Olive Garden in 1982. In June of 1995, General Mills spun off its restaurant division into Darden Restaurants, Inc. Today the Darden Group owns many restaurant chains, such as Olive Garden, Red Lobster, Bahama Breeze, and Smoky Bones. Olive Garden is one of the most famous and widespread chains of family restaurants focusing on the Italian dining experience. In a comfortable, home-like setting, guests receive warm, friendly service. Olive Gardens are known for fresh, quality Italian food, complemented by a great glass of wine.

Olive Garden's high quality service can be attributed to the training and development of restaurant employees. The company's annual training investment has increased five-fold in the past four years. As part of its employee culture, Olive Garden sends culinary managers to the Culinary Institute of Tuscany for training throughout the year to find new Italian dishes. In addition, Olive Garden hosts an annual wine ambassador trip to the vineyards of Italy. The result for Olive Garden guests is an enjoyable Italian dining experience.

Olive Garden is also involved in community development. It has partnerships with several organizations, including America's

Second Harvest, the nation's largest charitable hunger relief organization, and the Leukemia and Lymphoma Society.

Websites: Darden group: http://www.dardenrestaurants.com/
Olive garden: http://www.olivegarden.com/

Questions: How does the Olive Garden establish a "strategic difference" from the many restaurants competing for its business?

CASE 10: PENNSYLVANIA LIQUOR CONTROL BOARD

The sale, distribution and control of liquor is an important issue for every state government. The Pennsylvania General Assembly created Pennsylvania Liquor Control Board (PLCB) in 1933 to serve the public interest and its mission of regulation, retail sales and customer service, and alcohol education. PLCB has made recent changes to its distribution of self service state liquor stores (initiated 30 years ago). They recently opened the first One Stop Shop, a store within a supermarket. It is a full-scale store, operated by the PLCB, with more than 2,600 premium wine and spirits products and accessories. Other recent initiatives included the introduction of Sunday sale hours, the opening of six outlet stores, in-store tasting, the sale of accessories, an exclusive wine club, and the launching of an E-Commerce website featuring more than 1,700 premium wines, spirits, accessories and gift items.

PLCB has partnered with the private sector to create citywide wine festivals, beginning in Philadelphia in 2002, expanding to Pittsburgh in 2003 and most recently coming to Harrisburg. Pennsylvania was the first state to implement electronic license renewals for 18,500 licensees and permit holders. Licensees are now able to place their wine and spirits orders through the Internet. A major goal is to improve the overall licensed business experience via regulatory change and streamlining of operations (including online ordering and application submissions). PLCB offers alcohol education programs and resources for youth education through youth alcohol awareness programs, programs with colleges and universities, and programs to train employees on proper carding techniques.

Website: PA liquor control board: http://www.lcb.state.pa.us/
        Questions: With the agency becoming increasingly business-oriented, what is the vision of the PLCB's future-public agency or private contractor?

Part 2

LESSONS OF DESIGN & METHODS

Once beyond strategic planning's purpose, philosophy and concept, we confront the practical problems of steps and methods. What lessons are to be learned from the following questions:

- Who is to participate?
- What are the subjects?
- What is the role of the planner?
- Where and when will the planning be done?
- How much data will we use?
- What are its costs?
- Will the executive lead, follow or be absent?

In my experience, planning systems often fail because of basic flaws in the design, not because of recalcitrant staff. Although the participants are interested in the planning process and anxious to contribute, planning structure characteristics become problematic. These considerations can include the presence or absence of practical techniques and the lack of recognition that planning methodologies and approaches have come a long way since their early introductions. There are questions of strategic choice, including the resourcing of future products and services and the linkage of strategic visions to ongoing budgets and personnel responsibilities.

In this second part I have identified lessons to be learned in three areas:

- Lessons of planning system design
- Lessons of planning techniques
- Lessons of strategies and programs

These lessons will help the reader design more effective strategy formation processes from a methodological and practical point of view.

LESSONS OF PLANNING SYSTEM DESIGN

The first lesson in this set addresses a most basic and common error. It is ironic that planners forget to plan their own process.

PLAN TO PLAN

Lesson 12: The planning group never identified the beginning, the middle and the end.

All planning processes need a start. Participants require if not a road map at least "a sense" of the planning process, including how they will proceed, the resources they have to draw on, and the methodologies they will use. Although good planning processes are always ongoing, there are active and inactive phases. This requires that the planning group—including the chief executive and any outside consultants—create a plan to plan. One executive recommends addressing six questions in the design stages—addressing staff and member roles, data required, ownership and commitment, link to operational planning and capability for new initiatives.

The absence of a *plan to plan* is a silly error for planners to make. The common belief is that true planners hardly do anything without a plan. Yet some planners refuse to detail the steps in the process. These planners feel that the process should "just flow." In general I agree with the need for spontaneity but it is an error to let the process move in all directions at once as chaos and frustration result.

The reverse side of the no plan option is the elaborate creating of a planning recipe with accompanying bureaucracy. This is the error that too many organizations make as they create detailed planning manuals running 10-50 pages.

Illustration. In one federal agency—the Department of International Commerce—the senior director decided to initiate a strategic planning process. Both the director and the cabinet secretary were absolutely certain that the organization had become too bureaucratic. Strategic planning was intended to stimulate excitement and to open up long solidified departments to new ideas and new directions. They wanted a dynamic, people-driven process that would involve all levels of the organization at twenty-two national regional offices.

Unfortunately, the responsibility for the planning process was handed off to one of the deputy directors. He promptly decided to write an elaborate plan to plan—a recipe with beginning, middle and end. The key word here is elaborate. The document eventually produced was 45 pages long, complete with academic definitions, tables and charts. This planning manual was designed to be read by all planners in the 22 offices as well as critical managers and department heads.

Needless to say, very few people read the manual. But it did successfully announce to all members of the Department that the planning process would be a bureaucratic paper-driven one, with little in it for people.

After five years of successive iterations, managers, employees and technical staff scoff at the process.

SYSTEMS THINKING

Lesson 13: By only planning for the financial holes in our organization, we overlooked the company as a whole.

Systems thinking strategists for one organization had to address commercial requirements, politics, sports, entertainment, communications, transportation and security. Each aspect of their organization was interconnected so that performance in one of these "systems" had to be balanced with the needs of the others. Failure in any system would be instantly broadcast across the globe. What was the "company"—the organizing committee for the Atlanta Olympic Games.

Planning in the "old days" meant a focus on finances and the activities that produced and delivered the goods and services (e.g. engineering, marketing, customer services). To be effective, planning means planning for *all* of the organization—both its social and technical aspects. This "systems thinking" requires broader thinking including corporate culture, the way in which the organization is structured, the quality of working life and protection of human assets, and how managers manage—e.g. with participation or without. In short, this means planning "all over at once."

Several key points summarize this review of the connectedness of strategic planning and systems thinking.

- Strategic planning is social and technical in nature.
- The emphasis is on the whole and on the connectedness of parts with special attention also to processes not just outcomes.
- Focus of strategy is on the transformation of structure, process and outcomes to fit the desired future.
- The concept of entropy—strategy that is stationery is diminishing—is implied throughout the planning process.
- An internal process focus is appropriate but, "open systems" thinking through scanning and benchmarking means to look outside—even outside the subject industry.
- Contingency thinking—implies organizational uniqueness; meaning there is no "one best way" to craft strategy.
- Strategy formation is purposeful, planned and led in a manner that accounts for intended/rational and emergent/intuitive elements.
- Sometimes strategic attention is given to finance and to new products because they are more certain. Finances are quantifiable. Production systems and new products are tangible. Culture and executive behavior as strategic subjects are both abstract and introductions to personal change, stimulating avoidance in strategy formation. Professors Killing and Fry have presented the "whole organization" problem.

[Strategy] ... is being delivered by today's managers, rooted in today's corporate culture and reinforced by today's organizational setup. Getting tomorrow's strategy into place requires basic changes in management behavior and all of its supporting elements. Success depends on everything from developing new capabilities and systems to overcoming the inertia and resistance inherent in any break from the status quo.

Illustration. An insurance broker—the John Thompson Agency -was still close to its start up—founded only about four years earlier. The organization was struggling toward profitability, although it was making good progress in developing its products and services, facilities and structure. But the corporate board was beginning to press the executive for stronger progress on the financial bottom line. In discussions with outside advisors the chief executive talked about the need for a strategic review at this point in the new company's history.

As the advisor and the executive began to talk about the nature and process of a strategic appraisal, it was clear that the executive had in mind talking about how the products, services and facility might change and about how the board might change, but not about how the *executive* might change. The senior manager was planning for many parts of the organization but not all. Planning all over at once means that senior executives, managers and board members must plan for their own behaviors as well. Planning systems target *all* facets of the organization.

Note(s)
Killing, J.P.; Fry, J.N. "Delivering the Vision." *Business Quarterly*. Summer 1990, p. 49.

FIT WITH THE CULTURE

Lesson 14: Social butterflies do not vacation on deserted islands just as open planning does not work in closed corporate cultures.

This lesson targets the degree of fit between the planning and strategy formation system and the corporate culture. If the organization has traditionally operated as a closed group—with the future defined by a small set of executives at the top—it is unlikely that an open participative strategic planning system will be very successful. Wide involvement in planning the future is not used everywhere. Small closed groups can and do create dynamic and successful futures. However, the planning system must be designed to fit with the culture as it is, not as we would like it to be.

At least one exception to this process is worth noting. Some designers of planning processes use the development of a more open planning system as part of a strategy for changing the culture. By opening up planning and strategy formation—by involving more managers and employees in the creation of the future—culture change is initiated. Organizations experience both conflict and uncertainty when a traditionally closed, non-sharing culture engages in open dialogue about alternative futures.

Conversely, the organization that has historically been very open about its direction for the future and very involving of its employees and managers would have difficulty making a secretive planning process successful. Closed planning would be viewed as a violation of cultural norms and values. Employees have learned that the creation of the future is a "joint venture" of executives, managers and employees. Only unwillingly will they relinquish control to a small group of leaders.

Illustration. While advising a university hospital, the designers of the planning system took seriously the senior executive's interest in creating an open participative planning process. Without too much discussion of the nature of the culture, the consulting strategists developed a planning structure that included an advisory board and a series of task forces with board members and staff from all levels of the hospital's operations.

As the process began, the chief executive expressed greater and greater concern about the loss of control over the vision of the Waltham Medical Center's future. Repeatedly he asked the planners for assistance in getting the board members and staff in the task forces "back on track." He felt they were off creating a future that did not agree with his own vision.

As the consulting advisors discussed the executive's request, the nature of the fit between the planning system and the executive's concerns was confronted. It was clear that the organization had historically been run by a few people from the board and the senior staff. To his credit the executive quickly realized what he was asking for, perhaps somewhat unconsciously. He viewed the planning process (and was using the advisors) as part of an organizational change strategy, moving the Waltham Medical Center to a more open culture that relied on collaboration and teams. But this required that he change as well.

The year long planning process was very successful in involving many members of the organization in creating the future. It moved the hospital away from its historically closed culture in which all decisions were made at the top.

FORMALITY

Lesson 15: Following the details and the footnotes undercuts the flash and the flow of strategy formation.

Some planning processes are so formal that they impede creativity and excitement. The purpose of this book is to increase the process efficiency and the overall effectiveness of formal planning. An increase in formality alone can enhance planning productivity. But formality should be thought of as a process design characteristic that is on a continuum from more to less.

Many of us know entrepreneurs with nonexistent planning processes. Far from the large bureaucracy, there appears to be no strategic futures process at all. The very success of the entrepreneur indicates that formality is not a necessary characteristic of strategy formation. They craft the future without formal process.

Formal planning processes are characterized by graphs, charts, prepared reports distributed before the meetings, and very tightly controlled agendas. Yet, in other organizations external scanning, new directions and proposals for products and services are floated around the breakfast table at infrequent meetings. Flash and creativity are often present at the breakfast site. But informality with intuitive ideas floated in fast and loose fashion would be disparaged in large organizations.

The lesson here requires that we test the degree of fit between the formality that already exists in the organization and the formality of the strategic planning and strategy system.

Illustration. The question of "how formal" is best illustrated by planning in a federal government facility—the Food and Drug Safety Center. Because planning was recognized by the executives as one way that the organization could begin to influence its future, it made a decision to create a planning process. The Center was relatively large—about two thousand employees with an annual budget of approximately $100 million. Planning was historically driven by its budgeting process. The new planning system was designed to generate vision, some creativity about new services and excitement about the organization's future.

The planning advisor was somewhat surprised to find so strong an insistence on a formal agenda at the first meeting with the 26-person planning advisory board. After discussing possible planning procedures for two hours, the group adjourned. The advisor was even more surprised by one result of the first meeting. After agreeing that minutes would be taken in the first session, the minutes duly appeared at the second meeting—all twelve single spaced pages.

The twenty-six members of the planning group spent the first forty-five minutes clarifying and detailing corrections to the minutes, destroying all enthusiasm and pace.

This level of formality is defined as an error in design and approach.

TOP DOWN & BOTTOM UP

Lesson 16: Some say brilliant strategy floats up. Others say it flows down. Both directions are needed.

There is debate about whether strategic planning and strategy formation should be a top down or a bottom up process. Academics, consultants and public and private leaders argue about whether strategic directions and visions of the future should be driven by a small group of executives at the top, or "bubbled up" from the bottom by creative employees and managers. This debate seems to waste the time of all concerned.

If we truly believe that a vision of the organization's future is to be jointly created by all of its members, then the process requires both top down and bottom up thinking. Ideally there will be a comfortable degree of fit between where senior managers think the organization should go and where employees would like to go. However, even if there is a dispute, the learning by both sides can be strong. Learning through debate occurs because it is unlikely that either employees or managers will take the organization to a future they do not agree with. To plan *only* top down *or* bottom up is an error.

Illustration. At Midwestern Medical School the dean employed the top down approach to planning. Each year he and several senior associate deans met to decide where the school was going and what needed to be done. Although somewhat group oriented, the vision of the future was mostly created by the dean. Midwestern Medical School during this period made very rapid and successful progress in its development adding substantially to its patient care, teaching and research activities. But as the leadership changed, those in charge felt there was a need for a change in the design of the planning and strategy system.

As more and more physicians, faculty, employees and students became interested in the future of the school, they directly and indirectly asked for an opportunity to be a part of the process. Several decades into the history of the organization, the leadership began to include a bottom up approach to strategic planning. Executives did not ignore their responsibilities, but they did begin to match traditional top down directives with bottom up considerations. This change signaled to managers and employees that their ideas and opinions were important in planning Midwestern's future.

CHIEF EXECUTIVE OFFICER INVOLVEMENT

Lesson 17: The leader was missing—before, during and after the strategy sessions.

How involved should the chief executive be in the planning process? This question often comes up in the design phase and is one of the likely areas for error. Depending on the chief executive's notion of his or her responsibilities, the level of involvement is high or low.

For example, if the CEO believes that the role of the executive is to start the process but then delegate it to the planning team, involvement is likely to be minimal. If the CEO believes that the organization's plan for the future is his or her personal vision, then the CEO is likely to be very much involved and may dominate the process. When the CEO feels that planning is a joint effort by senior managers, then the involvement will vary at different points of the process but is continuous throughout.

Some of the writers in the strategic planning literature point out that those CEOs who regard involvement as unnecessary neglect one of the most critical responsibilities of their senior executive position. That is, to be uninvolved is not really an option. It is a dereliction of duty. Hamel and Prahalad are clear about the significant commitment.

> Our experience suggests that to develop a prescient and distinctive point of view about the future, a senior management team must be willing to spend 20% to 50% of its time over a period of months. It must then be willing to continually revisit that point of view, elaborating and adjusting it as the future unfolds.

The bottom line here is one of balance. The CEO provides visible leadership, support and enough involvement to be intimately involved in the process without wrecking it by dominating the debates and decisions.

Illustration. At the Tri-State Secondary School Council the CEO decided that a strategic planning process would be helpful to creating the future of the organization in what were defined as increasingly turbulent times for educators. The council executive felt that the process would help the organization define its direction and core service and said so in numerous staff meetings prior to the start up of planning. Senior managers and board members felt that the executive was leading an activity that would be beneficial to the organization.

The executive particularly felt that his role was to "get the planning started." That is just what he did, writing a very effective letter to all staff and board members, following up with an inspiring talk at the kickoff meeting of the planning group. Unfortunately, the chief executive never attended another meeting.

The impact of this level of CEO involvement was to undercut the process. His non-presence signaled that strategic planning could be disregarded and that strategy formation, if it occurred, happened elsewhere.

Note(s)
Hamel, G.; Prahalad, C.K. "Seeing the Future First" Book Excerpt Fortune, Sept. 5, 1994. From *Competing for the Future*. Cambridge, MA. Harvard Business School Press, 1994.

THE BOSS IS PRESENT

Lesson 18: The process was designed, outcomes were defined, but the executive did not even mail in an absentee ballot.

Often an executive will decide that they need a more formal strategic planning process. These leaders are so "personally involved" that they delegate the responsibility for creating the process to a vice-president, hire an outside consultant to create the planning design, and then expect the external facilitators to lead the process, write up the results and present the final product.

In some companies this approach is thought to be an efficient use of senior executive time. Unfortunately it is misplaced efficiency. To design an effective process and to generate a shared understanding of the expected outcomes, the executive must be intimately involved.

Since there are often wide differences between what a chief executive may expect from a strategic planning process and what managers and employees expect, it is necessary to come to a shared understanding at the outset. When the CEO is present to co-design the process, there is a greater surety that the planning system designed is one the leader can live with and even appreciate.

Importantly, the lesson includes the option for the executive to design a planning process whereby he is not present in a good number of the sessions. Some bosses are strongly assertive—tending toward the domineering. They overwhelm groups with their ideas and energy. While this is an excellent asset to the organization, it can inhibit the planning process. When the planning system is relatively new and when the culture involves a top down orientation from a tightly controlled executive group, the planning process must be carefully structured to avoid the dampening effect. If the boss is willing to talk openly about his or her role in the upcoming process, that communication may lead to minimizing his presence in key planning sessions where ideas are being solicited.

Illustration. We already reviewed a case in which the executive was only present for the initial meeting of the planning group the Tri-State Secondary School Council. Although that executive was involved in the planning system design, apparently the design discussions did not include an understanding of his role *throughout* the process.

In one department at Western University Law School, the strong willed chairman tended to make all of the decisions herself. Shouldering the responsibility for management, she freed her staff for legal teaching, practice and research. She intended to use the planning process to open up the department and decided that one way to do it was to minimize her involvement in the meetings. This executive signaled very clearly that she wanted new ideas. She supported the process but minimized her presence in order to ensure that the department faculty felt comfortable in contributing. This meant involvement at the first meeting of the planning group, at periodic sessions, the whole faculty retreats and at the wrap up sessions. At the conclusion she made the presentation of her plan both within the department and to other departments.

CEO RESPONSIBILITY

Lesson 19: Everyone knew planning was the CEO's responsibility—unfortunately, no one told the CEO.

Within the CEO's role in designing the strategy formation process is the critical responsibility for the development of the future. While some CEOs reserve all vision building work for themselves and their key associates, other CEOs do not recognize that the creation of the future is their responsibility. Future thinking is not an additional responsibility for the CEO, it is a *core* responsibility. Some CEOs talk about the time wasting burdens of planning processes. However, when these CEOs complain about the lack of return on their investment in planning time, they are talking about personal failure. It is an executive responsibility to plan for the organization's products, services, structure, culture, and managerial systems of tomorrow. When executives or boards define planning as a waste of time, they are admitting to a major failure of one aspect of their own work.

Illustration. Sometimes accepting planning is more than some CEOs can bear. One participant in strategic planning for a major consumer products company learned this lesson. The strategic planning process at Packer Company had been budget driven and bureaucratic in nature until they broke with tradition to hold a first planning retreat. The designers of the retreat decided that a strengths/weaknesses analysis would open up the process, move more toward a sense of vision and direction and away from budget-driven extrapolations of the past.

Unfortunately, no one informed the CEO that a critique of organizational strengths and *weaknesses* included the downside of leadership. When the group started criticizing the leaders, the CEO ended the retreat on the spot. He was apparently unwilling to confront the reality of his less-than-perfect organization. Although the planners were well on the way to attacking some problems—by first identifying them openly—the CEO did not understand it was his responsibility in the planning process to support confronting and discussing weaknesses.

PLANNER IDENTIFIED

Lesson 20: We agreed to plan, but we neglected to appoint a planner.

As if by magic, planning is supposed to occur without a personal sponsor or individual leadership. While the chief executive is ultimately responsible for strategy formation, someone in the organization must be identified as the strategy coordinator. The role of strategy planner varies from plan "developer" to "facilitator" of the process. The *developer* actually conducts the external and internal analyses and spends significant time creating alternative scenarios of the future. The development of the strategic plan itself is this planner's responsibility.

The strategy *facilitator* spends nearly all of his or her time *facilitating* the planning by managers, executives and employees in the organization. This planner's responsibility is the design and implementation of the strategy planning process.

These are very different ideas of the planner's role in the organization. Whichever role is chosen we must first agree that a planner must be identified. To the extent that the planning activity is added to someone's already existing set of responsibilities, it may not receive very much attention. Only if the strategist is made to understand that planning is a major contribution to the organization's development will he invest the time and energy required to make the strategy process a successful one.

In large organizations there is often a strategy planning staff. So the question is not one of is a planner identified but what is the role of the planner (see Lesson 21). Smaller organizations and professional groups rarely have standing planning staffs. The question of who is the identified planner then assumes much more importance as noted in the example below.

Illustration. In the fields of accounting, medicine, law and consulting, groups of privately practicing professionals are gradually growing larger. Often beginning with three to ten professionals, these practices develop to the point where planning for the practice future is a critical need. The staff work on critical aspects of practice activity from projects to scheduling to billing to client relations. Planning skills and experience are rarely present. Therefore, identifying the planner is important for small private professional groups.

For example, a small clinical group with five profesionals—Surgery Associates—decided that they were becoming large enough to begin to systematically consider the development of their future. In a group session they agreed that someone needed to initiate the planning process. They quickly realized that no one—including their practice manager—had been through a process before and none of the partners felt they had the confidence to undertake the task. The group elected to hire an outside consultant to guide them. The strategy planning consultant facilitated the planning process and educated the group members on the nature and methods of planning. The planner identified in this case was a technical expert, facilitator and a planning educator and was from outside the practice. To continue planning, the practice manager has been assigned the responsibility with the freedom to call on the consultant for assistance.

THE PLANNER ROLE

Lesson 21: The board and the planner agreed that the planner was there to create the plan—but they were wrong.

As the planner is being identified—the organization must address the role. As noted above, roles vary from that of plan creator (the "thinker upper" of the future) to that of designer and facilitator of the planning activity of managers and executives. It is my view that the most effective "planner role" is as designer and facilitator of planning by experienced executives and managers. The role is process design and facilitation but not strategy selection.

Planners function successfully in both role sets. In some major private companies such as GE, both internal and external planners are used to conduct analyses and to create alternative scenarios for the organization. In other organizations the development of ideas and vision is thought to be the responsibility of the board, the executives, managers and employees. The role for the planner is to assist and support the development and communication of ideas and visions by the *members* of the organization. The contribution of industry specific analysis and involvement in the choice of strategic directions, products and services is minimal.

The misunderstanding of the role here is a major error. If the board or senior management thinks they have hired someone to create a vision of the organization's future, they will be mightily disappointed when "all they receive" is assistance in the process. They will have retained the responsibility for planning themselves—which is precisely the point with the facilitator model. As a turnabout, this is procedural reinforcement of a philosophical point about the design of effective planning. Many executives, board members and planners feel that the best creators of the organization's future are members of the organization themselves, not outsiders or strategy specialists.

Illustration. In one of the early meetings at the Eastern Medical Society, there was a brief confrontation with the chairman of the board over the confusion in roles. The planning consultant understood that he was there to design a planning process that would help the society move toward a desired future. The chairman of the board appeared confused on two points. First, *he* understood-mistakenly-that the planner was to create the organization's future in scenario form. His words were: "You will write up what we tell you if you want to be paid." He wanted to let the planning consultant know quite clearly that the future would be driven by the board. The planning consultant was not to go far afield with his own version of the society's future.

Second, the chairman wondered whether the planner could assist the organization quickly and be done, with not too much time involved. It was clear that the chairman misunderstood the role of the planner and the time requirements attached to the role of designer and facilitator of the strategy formation process. The planner was eventually involved in the entire planning process, but not in the scenario and future building work. The quick version of "contracted out, once and done planning" was not followed. It was replaced by an ongoing internal planning effort that lasted for several years.

PLANNER ORIENTATION

Lesson 22: Some planners count everything; some planners engage people; some planners do both.

In strategic planning practice, there is a split between those who see planning as an effort to quantify everything and those who see planning as an effort to engage and motivate employees. While in principle we have advocates at both ends of the spectrum, in practice we would hope to see a combination of measurement and engagement. Numbers-oriented planners begin with measurement of all aspects of the organization. Sooner or later they confront the complexity of selecting and analyzing various measures. But they continue to emphasize documentation and numbers. People-oriented planners feel movement toward a desired future is driven by values, mission and personal commitment. Teambuilding and collaboration are key, much more important than "the numbers." In practice, the quantitative planners ignore the social system side while the people planners want to "feel good without measuring." Neither will work without the other.

Illustration. Consider two widely known corporate examples in the news—Enron and Anderson accountants. If we could have listened in on the strategic planning exercises five or 10 years ago, what would we have heard? A discussion of market share, revenues and profit margins would certainly have been on the agenda. But would integrity, core values and representation to the greater public have been part of the strategic review? Enron leaders would subsequently reward margins and profitability, exempting concern for honesty and fair dealings in the market place. Their accounting firm —Anderson—was drawn into the strategy, neglecting client and professional values in favor of revenues and returns. Was the outcome—the demise of both companies—the desired future crafted in their strategic planning sessions? I think not.

THE PLANNER'S AUTHORITY

Lesson 23: The planner believed he had an important role, but everyone knew he never once saw the CEO.

How does the planner establish the authority to carry out the planning role? Aspects of the planning process require that the planner coordinate and organize the activities of senior executives in the organization, managers at various levels throughout the organization and employees that do not report to him or her. Relying on coercion, some planners are tempted to use their position to "order people around"—an effective method for *short* tenure.

The most successful planners seem to rely on a different power base. They expect planning to be effective when they exert planning power based on *personal charisma* and *esteem*, *knowledge* of the planning process, and *referent* power based on their reporting relationship to the chief executive officer. Threats of coercion and loss of rewards rarely work as inducements to participation in the planning process. The relationship with top management is critical.

To whom the planner reports is an important indicator of the level of the support for planning and it reveals strategy formation assumptions. The planner should report to the chief executive but another senior executive with strong informal authority is also common. When the planner reports to a lower level officer or to an obscure division, the "message" is obvious. If planning were truly important, a critical senior person would have oversight responsibility. For example, when the planner reports to a senior vice-president for human resources it suggests that planning is seen as a people and communication-driven process. Alternatively, reporting to the financial officer would suggest that the planning done will be financial in nature, will be quantitative and will be oriented toward the bottom line as a major indicator of success.

Illustration. In the State Environmental Affairs Agency, planning and policy making were cited as critical aspects of the organization—in the words of the cabinet secretary. However, in practice, the policy and planning group reported most often to a special assistant who reported to a special assistant who reported to the Secretary of the Department. The special assistant wielded little power within the organization either by virtue of expertise or by virtue of formal position. As deputy secretaries and department heads came to understand that the policy and planning group had no special relationship to their senior executive, the planning group's authority to effectively control and organize the strategy planning process was eliminated.

PLANNING COMMITTEE

Lesson 24: The planning committee had a cast of thousands. We never understood what they were supposed to do.

In many private companies and public agencies a committee is used to design the planning process, to craft a plan with vision and strategy, to monitor its progress through the various phases, and to evaluate the outcome. The development of the planning committee's purposes and membership is a key task in the plan-to-plan stage.

Most often errors are made by either involving too many people in the process, or conversely, by keeping the group too small. Research regarding small group behavior suggests that the best groups function in size from around 8 to 12 persons. In some cases larger groups work quite well, in other cases smaller groups function very effectively. But the core question of how big a planning committee should be is addressed mostly by the small group research.

There is one qualification to this guideline. With some planning systems, the size of the planning committee is determined by intent—to involve as many people as possible. The overriding purpose is involvement not planning management. In those designs there is often a small executive committee of 8 to 10 persons planning on a day-to-day basis. The error arises in mistaking one for the other.

By trying to use the executive group as a whole advisory committee, the need for participation and involvement of many persons is neglected. However, by attempting to push all day-to-day decisions through a very large group (such as 25 to 35 persons) the difficulties bog down in the practical problems of discourse and consensus.

One simple size related problem often neglected is that of "air time." The larger the group the smaller the amount of air time—contributed comments—for each of the participants. The planning designers may be interested in the involvement and consultative advice of many persons. But when 30 persons are in a room for a limited time, not everyone can talk about every issue. These "air time limits" created by size diminish both the involvement and contribution that were the goals of the large group size.

Illustration. At Middleburg Manufacturing the planning committee was formed with representation from many of the departments. The design principle was to use the planning committee as a technical advisory group to provide intimate current knowledge of the institution, as a source of historical background on the practice of planning to date, and to ensure representativeness of various departments. However, a contentious debate broke out in the early stages of planning.

Some organizers argued for a small group of eight persons. They suggested this was the only workable size for Middleburg's planning requirements which included both a rather short time frame and fairly significant decisions at a key point in company development. However, the size of the planning group quickly increased as a call for representation from all of the product lines was heeded. This necessitated some 10 to 12 department heads becoming part of the team as a base group. When a few of the executives and senior managers were added, the group quickly went to 20. After the first meeting, the group was criticized for not including key functional departments. Within six months their representatives were added so that the "small planning group" floated to 26. At the annual retreat there were 35 persons in attendance including staff assistants to some of the senior managers.

While the group functioned, it was far from the small group envisioned at the start of the process.

CONSULTANTS

Lesson 25: This organization uses no consultants. "We can do it all," the board chairman said arrogantly.

Consultants are a much maligned group. Many managers criticize both their cost and their contribution while others defend their usefulness and continue to employ them. The question of whether to engage consultants raises several assumptions about the participants' view of their organization and about leaders' ability to plan.

First, leaders' use of consultants offers a clue to the corporate culture. A statement that no outsiders are used—*ever*—reveals that the board and senior managers feel that they are knowledgeable about every aspect of both internal operations and external relations. This position is frequently attacked as a major weakness by many organization thinkers and executives. Internal operations and external environments are increasingly too complex and dynamic for all knowledge to be available within the company.

Second, the position that no consultants are used suggests that the organization is so successful at planning that no outsiders are needed to assist them in developing and maintaining their high level of planning capability. This, too, is infrequently the case. While there are surely persons with the skills inside the organization to create scenarios, to facilitate the process and to follow-up on the planning agenda, the presence of outsiders frequently signals the importance of the work, the need to include additional expertise, fresh ideas about futures and the usefulness of a referee at certain points in the process.

Many organizations use consultants: (1) to assist in the design of the strategic planning process; (2) to facilitate sessions; (3) to provide outside appraisal of environmental trends and strategic decisions; and (4) to provide trouble-shooting advice when planning seems to be struggling. The most common use of consultants is in design of the planning process and facilitation of strategy planning sessions. Consultants work in many industries and different types of organizations and can transfer successful planning technology from one organization to another.

While internal facilitators can lead the organization through sorting out company strengths, when weaknesses are discussed everyone squirms. Consultants are particularly useful when conducting an internal analysis of strengths and weaknesses. The presence of a neutral facilitator who is supportive enough to encourage thoughtful, constructive analysis of the organization's downside is easily worth the expenditure.

Illustration. In many universities outside facilitators are used to assist academic departments that have their own experts in planning and organizational development. For the same reasons that physicians and lawyers and health care executives cannot conduct an objective internal appraisal, faculty in a business school also would be incapable of facilitating the dialogue within their own department, even though they have the skills to do so and apply them on the outside. It is precisely the position of the "outsider" that enables the process.

As a second example, consider the reaction in the Gannett newspaper chain to an announcement that a daily newspaper would be created on the Internet. Many veteran reporters and newspaper executives would quickly downplay the competitive threat. However, since the idea was announced by Microsoft, some attention is warranted. Strategy Consultants International could be hired by the newspaper chain to evaluate the plausibility of this new product, including technical capabilities, time to start up, expected market share and impact on the newspaper chain worldwide.

NUMBER OF PARTICIPANTS

Lesson 26: First we had forty planners, then only one. Neither amount was correct.

How many executives, managers and employees should participate in the planning process? Although seemingly simple, this is a critical question of planning system design. This error is an extension of the planning committee size problem (see Lesson 24). For those executives and commentators who believe in open participative planning, the answer is easy—involve high numbers of participants. If planning is viewed as an open, shared process that is the task of many individuals within the organization, the planning participants can range from the tens to the hundreds. *How* they are organized is the question that concerns designers of planning systems, not how their numbers can be restricted.

Here we are back to the question of planning philosophy addressed in Part I. If planning for the organization's future is seen primarily as an exclusive task of senior management—a small group of four to six—then the number of participants is an easy question. The planners are senior executives, period.

If, however, the philosophy of planning involves a participative process that encourages commitment to a shared vision of the future, then it is necessary to involve large numbers of managers, board members and employees.

In choosing the number of participants, a second point of planning system assumptions is surfaced. When one holds the number of participants to a very few—four to six, for example—then one assumes that those four to six persons are up to the task. They are able to do an excellent job of assessing the organizational environment; of analyzing the internal strengths and weaknesses; of constructing a vision of the future; and of identifying strategies, programs and actions to attain the future. Conversely, an expanded number of participants admits that complex organizations operating in complex environments require large numbers of persons to conduct the analysis and to create and realize the future.

Illustration. On one of the two campuses of a private university, the provost initiated a campus level strategic planning process in conjunction with the university's overall planning process. Although the planning process at the campus level could have been a small and somewhat limited initiative, the provost instead chose high involvement.

Some 18 task forces were formed on a campus with only 300 faculty and 9500 students. The formation of the task forces and the high number of participants (7 to 10 persons per task force with both faculty and outside representatives) was intended to signal to the academic community that the issues were complex, that multiple inputs were needed, and that all of the academic community was involved in the creation of the college's future.

While participation of this scale is somewhat unwieldy and presents difficulties in planning system management, the philosophy of participation and the desire to include all members in the creation of the future has very strong advantages such as diversity of ideas and commitment to the vision.

PARTICIPANTS' ROLES

Lesson 27: Strategy "thinkers" should be the "do-ers."

Early efforts at strategic planning often used strategy groups located at headquarters. These teams were charged with the responsibility of inventing strategies that would be successful in the field. Operations executives were "implementers" of strategy devised by strategists who were divorced from the demands of operations. Isolated strategists often created strategies that were ill-suited to actual product, service and market demands. We still have this problem in some companies, but many have solved the "lack of reality" by incorporating operations managers into the strategic planning process. The presence of these "do-ers" brings experience and new ideas into the somewhat sterile strategy making process.

Illustration. In the Middleton School District, administrative leaders quickly responded to the "No Child Left Behind" federal education law by mandating that teachers be certified in all fields in which they teach courses. Building Principals would lead the process building by building. This general strategy at the local level seemed to fit the purpose of increasing the quality and preparation of the teaching staff. But the administrators neglected to see the problems of cost and timing of certification, the grandfathering in of current teachers and the complex bureaucratic processes used to issue the certifications. Principals that were responsible for their teachers saw the problems instantly but these implementers were not involved in the central office strategizing.

LOCATION

Lesson 28: There were two choices for the location of the planning retreat: the CEO's office, or the Islands Social and Boating Club— neither was appropriate.

The choice of location for strategic planning retreats, and for the other sessions of the planning process, is one of those practical, seemingly simple, but exceedingly difficult problems. Most planners decide to ensure that the planning group is off by itself for some block of time, if not on a regular basis. This means that the planning system designers must begin to choose between types and levels of sites available. The choice brings up a host of considerations including travel time, travel expense, total cost, type of facilities and expectations of the participants.

For example, planning that occurs in the chief executive's office is likely to be exceedingly intimidating to the participants. Sitting in his or her office, it is difficult to suggest ideas that run counter to prevailing philosophy or actions. Few planners choose the CEO's office as a site, but some get very close, e.g. the adjoining board room.

Most often planners choose an external location for the retreat as a part of the "planning to plan" process when many design issues are discussed. The choices are determined by the resources available. Private companies use expensive vacation or convention center sites. Longer travel times are chosen in order to give the participants an opportunity to talk informally with each other to and from the retreat site, but some participants complain about travel time.

The more luxurious surroundings detract from the time commitment and the seriousness of the planning process. When planning participants see that golf, boating, tennis, and beach time are easy alternatives, their focus weakens. There are a great many facilities that offer compromise, not quite an elaborate vacation spot, but well beyond the local hotel's conference room.

Illustration. In many retreats over the past thirty years, I have experienced planning processes in very luxurious surroundings and in very simple ones. I am not convinced that the surround has all that much to do with the effectiveness of the planning. For example, one professional group conducted their annual planning retreat at a very expensive spa. Participants generally were engaged in the planning process for half to two-thirds of the day, taking advantage of the spa's recreational and health services for the remainder of the time.

Another retreat used a federal education and training center. The center was Spartan in its facilities. The hotel rooms were dormitory style while the dining facility was a cafeteria. All meeting rooms were set up as classrooms, equipment was in place and the food was exceedingly good. This training center at a remote location required six hours of travel by bus so participants had an extended opportunity to talk.

A third example involved a retreat by a small community services organization. They too wanted to get away for at least an overnight, but resources were tight. They located a religious retreat center that provided quite comfortable surroundings with home cooked, family style meals. Facilities for ping-pong and trails for hiking in the woods were quite adequate for break times during the very effective planning process.

QUANTITATIVE ORIENTATION

Lesson 29: The analyses were clear to all participants, at least those with expertise in regression analysis.

Some years ago, it was quite common to find very quantitatively-oriented strategic plans. This was the remnant of the first phase of strategy formation when strategic planning was defined as synonymous with financial planning. Since finances are amenable to quantitative analysis, it was easy to convert financial thinking to numbers—driven strategic planning.

At the far end of the spectrum of planning methodologies it was hoped that computer models and quantitative analysis would provide stunningly precise analysis and lead, via formula, to clear strategic directions for the organization. Unfortunately the world intervened, making environments much more complex than financial analysis could handle.

Additionally, as our thinking about the nature of strategic planning evolved from a narrow view to a more broadly defined systems view, a quantitative orientation was considered to be necessary but not sufficient for the whole strategic analysis process.

Summarizing earlier work on management information with regard to strategy Mintzberg notes:

1. Hard information is often limited in scope, lacking richness and often failing to encompass important non-economic and non-quantitative factors....
2. Much hard information is too aggregated for effective use in strategy making....
3. Much hard information arrives too late to be of use in strategy making....
4. Finally, a surprising amount of hard information is unreliable.

Private corporations with their focus on the bottom line led the way with quantitative business analysis. But they have now pushed the methodology further, a more balanced analysis that includes fuzzier concepts such as culture, management style, and quality of working life. These internal corporate structure and people dynamics issues are now a part of mainstream planning, as are the more difficult to quantify external issues such as shifts in cultural values and customer attitudes, and changes in life style.

Illustration. One banker, a graduate of a well-known school of business, applied financial analysis to all of Interstate Bank's activities. In talking to his board of directors about the direction for the bank and the strategies for attaining the future, the president stressed formulas for commercial success, particularly those forecasting quarterly and yearly results.

Unfortunately, the board members, who were very successful but relatively unsophisticated business men and women, did not understand the formulas and so discounted the analysis. Several experienced board members were aware that the banker was stressing finances and bottom line only. He was ignoring the need to establish strong customer ties for new business, and he was not developing the internal human resources to enable Interstate to function effectively in the future.

By using quantitative business analysis the banker neglected several other critical factors. The psychology of customers and employees, the building of a service oriented culture and a "marketing-oriented" management style were missing from the quantitative formulas. Until the planning process was broadened only part of Interstate Bank was affected by strategy formation.

Note(s)
Mintzberg, H. *The Rise and Fall of Strategic Planning.* New York: Free Press, 1994, p. 259-266.

QUALITATIVE ORIENTATION

Lesson 30: The planning document appeared to be the work of social workers, philosophers and fuzzy thinkers with rose colored glasses.

The flip side to the quantitative orientation is a complete focus on qualitative issues—what those with unkind thoughts call "soft and fuzzy" concepts. With this orientation, the planning group concentrates on the attitudes, perceptions, values and feelings side of the organization. These elements are far more difficult to quantify and to evaluate in terms of progress toward some desired future. This orientation is a welcome change from some of the earlier quantitative domination, but it has its own weaknesses.

McGrath and MacMillan summarized four common problems in tying information systems to planning:

- Companies don't have hard data but, once a few key decisions are made, proceed as though their assumptions are facts

- Companies have all the hard data they need to check assumptions but fail to see the implications
- Companies possess all the data necessary to determine that a real opportunity exists but make implicit and inappropriate assumptions about their ability to implement the plan
- Companies start off with the right data, but they implicitly assume a static environment and thus fail to notice until too late that a key variable has changed.

As strategists we tend to forget that it is possible to count and measure cultural, stylistic and psychological elements that indicate organizational progress, or the lack thereof. Using both qualitative and quantitative indicators, we can create mileposts by which the organization will be able to evaluate its progress toward the future.

The qualitative orientation as sole focus of strategy formation is an error often made by clinical and service agency leaders in the public sector. They measure their strategic progress for example in terms of patient care and access to services. Sometimes there is a "fallback" to the financial bottom line as an indicator, but it is usually accompanied by strong reservations, feelings that it is an inappropriate measurement tool. In other public agencies, outright conflict overwhelms the planning group. Money cannot be the sole measurement in service organizations such as hospitals, schools or professional practices.

To avoid both the quantitative and qualitative orientation errors balance the two approaches. Careful selection of the strategy group to ensure that there are persons representing both the quantitative and qualitative styles of thinking is one way to handle this problem.

Illustration. At a strategic planning retreat for professionals in the mental health field, the qualitative orientation was most dominant. The planners at Psychiatric Services Center wanted a sense of how their organization was affecting both their clients individually and their client group as a whole. However, measurement of mental health improvement is far from an exact science and is one of the most difficult measurement subjects of all. Any move to focus the discussion on financial data or administrative topics (e.g., patients served, therapy sessions provided) was resisted by the planning group. They argued about the need to have a "sense" of how each patient was progressing as a result of their treatment. They wanted to know whether their Center was making a difference in the lives of patients and their patient group in their region.

Planning in this case required feedback of a qualitative nature. Presentations of case successes and failures provided participants with a "feel" for their contribution and for the degree of progress their organization was making toward its desired future—high quality service to a geographically defined patient population. An assessment of patient demographic variables—age, sex, race, geographic origin, disease type—would also demonstrate whether the whole target population was being reached (a step toward qualitative-quantitative balance).

Note(s)
McGrath, R.G.; MacMillan, I.C. "Discovery-Driven Planning." Harv. Bus. Rev. Jul-Aug 1995; p. 46.

COMPUTERS

Lesson 31: The strategy group's offices quickly became known as MIT West. But when the modeling failed, the planners threw away their computers, which was also a bad idea.

There are two approaches to strategic planning and strategy formation, one quantitative, the other people oriented. The *cost and count* quantitative crowd of strategic planners believe computers should dominate because:

- numbers and hard analysis are the starting points
- measurement is key
- the lack of planning is costly
- planning must document progress in numbers
- measurement is complex
- number jockeys are required.

The *people* oriented crowd of strategic planners believe:

- mission and values are key
- big gains in organizational capability are not measured
- team work is the essence
- change bubbles up
- people are the starting point for vision and future.

Obviously computers are more valuable to the *cost and count* crowd.

The use of computers in the planning process is one of the hotly debated topics among planning academics, consultants and executives. At the start of a new century of high technology we cannot advocate a planning process devoid of computer support. However, an error allied to the obsession with quantitative approaches develops when computers are expected to think *for* the planning group. Planners feel that if they input numbers with the correct formulas, the computer produces both the strategic direction required for organizational success and the programs, actions and strategies needed to get the organization there. Those who have used computer models extensively are well aware of the difficulties of using the technology and of the fallacy of hoping that the computer will be the thinker. Thus, one part of this lesson ensures that the computer is used to *support* the thinking process of the *planners* as they move through strategic analysis. As Ackoff notes: "There is nothing about a management system that requires any part of it to be computerized; including strategic planning. Until computers can think, planners will have to."

A second part of the lesson addresses the heavy reliance on computers as a technological component of the planning process that is exceedingly time consuming, resource intensive and difficult to manage. Planning processes with tight time lines commonly experience the arrival of computer-generated data after the process has been completed. Other planners feel that the time and resources demands for information generation aspects of the planning require more than the whole planning process. Carefully controlling and effectively using computer produced data support is the objective.

Illustration. Perhaps the worst challenge to controlling computers involves planning in a computer company. At Zodiac Data Systems planners automatically moved toward simulations, impact models and computer language to talk about the future and the emerging program activities of their company. The dialogue was mostly hardware/software related. During strategy formation, it was important to move these high tech planners away from discussions of their technology—which quickly becomes a crutch—and toward inclusion of culture, business markets, customer attitudes, management style and quality of working life. To the extent that broader organizational issues can be addressed with computer based support, it is appropriate to stay technically based. Organizational issues in this kind of company are certainly related to computers as a technology, but the company requires discussions of issues beyond hardware/software configurations by technologically oriented people.

Note(s)
Ackoff, R.L. *Creating the Corporate Future*. New York: Wiley, 1981, p. 133.

TIME FRAME

Lesson 32: The organization completed their first planning process in two hours, the next one required two years; both were wrong.

How long should the planning process be? This simple question has no single answer. Commentators on planning believe the strategy process is continuous. However, most planning processes involve a series of phases—times when more *planning* activity occurs and other times with more implementation *action*, with *evaluation* at follow-up points. Many senior managers will push to keep the time investment to a minimum. Hamel and Prahalad dismiss this "light touch" directly.

> The half-day or day-long planning review meetings that typically serve as forums to debate the future are utterly inadequate if the goal is to build an assumption base about the future that is more prescient and better-founded than the competitors'.

In several decades of planning I have experienced "intensive processes" of approximately *four hours* and others that have taken 15 months. Some part of the "length-of-time" decision relates to the size of the organization. With 5,000-10,000 or more employees, it is difficult to conduct organization-wide planning in less than a significant period of time, e.g. six months to one year.

However, the large organization time period does not define the time requirements for small organizations or for entrepreneurial companies. In private professional practices or start up companies, the actual planning period cannot possibly take six months as the organization is concerned with survival and day-to-day productivity. Since survival is the key need of a new company, a planning process that lasts from 12 to 15 months may outlive the company.

Avoiding error means matching the nature of the organization with the time frame. A large public organization requiring citizen input and political negotiation requires speed on the part of all parties but will still require six months to a year. Entrepreneurs in planning processes requiring excessive numbers of meetings and document preparation are likely to grumble about the time commitment and, they will question the utility of the exercise.

One solution to this problem is to ask the planners about the time needed to complete the main part of the planning analysis, even as they think about it as an ongoing process.

Illustration. Leaders of a large federally administered hospital—Soldiers Memorial—might have been expected to take an exceedingly long time to move through the planning process. In first considering the process timeline, the judgment of the planning group was that months were needed (an estimate was 6-9). However, the physicians at Soldiers Memorial Hospital stressed that they have limited time to contribute to administrative tasks such as planning. Their position was that the main phase of the process—strategic analysis and creating the vision—could only last three months. Thus, 90 days was the time period structured by what key participants could commit to this part of the process.

In another example, a clinical department in a medical school determined that in order to meet the dean's requirements for submitting a plan, they had exactly 30 days. Since their patient care commitments were already exceedingly high, they voted to give approximately four hours a week for four weeks to the planning process. Admitting that later they may need to extend certain analytical studies and their vision, they decided that 30 days (with 16 hours of meetings) was the time they could give to the process. The limit forced efficiency and some contracting out of planning support.

Note(s)
Hamel, G.; Prahalad, C.K. "Seeing the Future First." Book Excerpt. Fortune. Sept 5, 1994; p.64. From *Competing for the Future*. Cambridge, MA: Harv. Business School Press, 1994.

PAPER VS. PROCESS PRODUCT

Lesson 33: The final plan was carried in "casket style" by 12 strong men.

How much paper is required to present the final plan? The real question here is do we regard strategic planning as a *process* comprised mostly of analytical debates and *dynamic discussion*? Or, do we think of the product as the *plan* at the end? For William French, Director of the Rural Community Assistance Center, the answer is clear: "Strategic planning is primarily a process. Surely when you get to the end there is a document that is essentially a recording of the process and decisions made along the way. But, in strategic planning, it is the process—the information, learning, considerations, and decisions—that are the most important."

Most often the error involves thinking that the output of the planning process is the written document. Many planning groups have spent hundreds of hours focusing on the production of paper. But the real output of planning is the discussion of the future by key leaders from all levels of the organization. We can think of the paper product as the *clerical* summary of the important work of the planning process—dialogue and decisions. A concise executive summary is all that is needed. Unfortunately, this is a lesson too often learned the hard way in both the public and the private sectors (with shelves of hundred page plans collecting dust as evidence).

Illustration. The emphasis on brevity in the final plan is best illustrated by a very old prestigious private university's experience in creating its strategic plan. The process required each of the 16 colleges in the university to submit a strategic plan at the start of the calendar year. As each college moved through their processes (many of which were productive and participative) they also created elaborate final documents. The central planners were excited about the success of the strategic planning process, but forgot to control for the "paper versus process problem." At the end of the year, each of the colleges submitted their plans (including science, engineering, arts and humanities, and so on.) Typically the college plans were from 100 to 150 pages as each Dean wanted to demonstrate that they had done their analytical "homework." When multiplied by 16, the number of pages in the collected document was stunningly large.

Needless to say, it was unusable. Executive summaries were prepared.

In a second example of the same lesson, the Danton School District prepared its strategic plan for its geographic region. Excited about the concept of strategic planning, the superintendent of schools, his staff and board members (the planning team) decided that the plan should be read by the full board and all faculty. Unfortunately, the team forgot that faculty and board members' reading time is scarce. The plan was delivered as a 180 page single spaced legal size document. Although there are no data on readership—very few people waded through the 180 pages. The intention—to communicate the exciting direction and future activities of the school district—was undercut by the density of the final planning document.

FACILITATOR

Lesson 34: The organization left the referee in the locker room, along with the starting gun and whistle.

Executives debate whether they need someone from the outside to assist them with the strategy planning process. The question is not raised because of the lack of group process skills or planning expertise within the organization. Instead the issue is do we need a guide who is separated from the politics and behavioral dynamics of the organization?

Even when a facilitator from inside the organization is acting in a neutral fashion, participants often perceive them to be an agent of the CEO, or a captive of various factions. This does not mean that any organization that selects a facilitator is racked with conflict. To the contrary, in excellent organizations, departments and subgroups vie for scarce resources and, in a constructive way, attempt to persuade the group as a whole that their vision of the future and strategies for getting there are the most useful. A facilitator can help the process by ensuring that both sides are debating fairly, openly and comprehensively. When the conflict rises to certain levels or extraneous issues are dragged in, the facilitator can signal a halt, support negotiation or change the direction of the discussion.

Facilitators are sometimes used solely for the retreats that are a typical part of the overall planning process. At other times they are used as process consultants to observe and support planning as the group moves from beginning to end. Since planning is one aspect of senior management responsibility, facilitators often provide feedback on general management style and behavior as well.

Some organizations still debate the need for a facilitator. But the increasing acceptance of facilitation by outsiders is a lesson seemingly learned by many public and private organizations.

Illustration. Facilitators are often most useful in guiding the group through the internal analysis of the organization. Most planning designs require some variation of a strengths/weaknesses analysis. Internal facilitators can easily guide the group through the analysis of strengths, but confronting weaknesses is a problem.

In the Property Protect insurance company—known for its turnover of employees and as a place not to work—senior executives began to conduct their strengths/weaknesses analysis in a strategic planning retreat. When the question of quality of working life at the company came up, one of the marketing vice-presidents suggested: "We may have a people problem in our organization."

Before he completed his sentence, the Vice-President for Human Resources said in rapid-fire fashion

"NOWEDON'T."

The Human Resources Vice-President was immediately defensive, launching the group into an argument that undercut the constructive identification of topics to be tackled in creating the company's desired future. After an hour of very tense argument, the CEO suggested the group table the concern for now. A facilitator would have helped the group through some further diagnosis of the internal climate.

COSTS

Lesson 35: A penny saved on strategy formation may cost £1,000 in future profit.

The cost of a strategy planning process is plotted on a very wide scale. Some organizations invest very minimally in their strategists and formal planning process. One of their existing staff devotes five percent of their work time each year to organizing and supporting the planning process. Staff costs are already budgeted; outside costs are nearly zero as all meetings are at the company offices.

Others—many major corporations—hire outside consultants, use outside retreat facilities and spend anywhere from several hundred thousand dollars to a million dollars or more on their planning.

The lesson has several parts. Unchecked spending does not guarantee success even with luxurious surroundings. Conversely, not investing any resources in the planning process is an indicator that the organization does not truly believe in formal strategy planning.

There are relatively few organizations in either the public or the private sector that believe they can be successful without any planning at all. When organizations begin a debate about the cost of the planning process deeper assumptions surface. Planning consultants may confront the issue by responding to an executive team's comment: "Costs are too high." The response: "What is it we are really talking about?."..."Are we truly concerned about the money or are we resisting the concept of more open formal planning?"

The cost debate is often an indicator of failed experiences. Vigorous reservations about cost are disguised concerns about the usefulness of planning. Too many organizations have learned that huge investments in external strategic analyses and consultants have limited payoffs. In some cases, the analyses are needed to generate openness to change and to stimulate interest in strategic alternatives. However, in other cases, the reports are massive documents placed on shelves with the hundred page plans and never read.

Illustration. The cost problem arises when executives contact planning design consultants to discuss a possible engagement. Invariably, the consultants hear this from executives;

"But we have no money budgeted for planning."

The response is straightforward: if there are no financial resources to be found to support planning, the organization is probably not very serious about a more formal strategy formation process separate from what they have been doing. Most organizations find the money and thereby reinforce their commitment to the process.

The one exception is that small public and non-profit organizations are truly short of resources for anything. In those cases, planning consultants and facilitators often cut their fees or provide the service as a volunteer. And it is possible to find donated retreat sites and volunteer analysts that will allow small service agencies to hold the costs of planning to low levels.

Strategy consultation costs in major private companies must be considered in perspective. At Ford Motor Company and General Motors internal strategists have been at work for years on the potential of third world markets. As some of the countries move forward investment in strategy advice is warranted. The cost of a two million dollar strategy study conducted in China is dwarfed by the potential return on investment in that country's huge population of future drivers. Leaders at Coca-Cola would feel the same way.

SIMPLICITY

Lesson 36: KISS—keep it simple stupid—is a cliché because many managers remember it. But some planners forget.

The error of lost simplicity is one that academics, planning consultants and some internal planners make quite easily. In pushing for comprehensiveness, planning system designers too frequently create a complex process that is very hard to make work in practice.

In my own experience, a simple and lean planning system de-emphasizes the steps and techniques of planning and emphasizes the dialogue between leaders of the organization. This is somewhat of a disappointment to planners who like all professionals become enamored of analytical methodologies, group process tools and phases in flow charts.

We are discussing a philosophical problem with planning known commonly as the means/ends trap. The purpose of planning is not to plan but to create the organization's future. Planning systems that are too elaborate or too long have substituted the means of planning for the ends of creating the future. Organizations do not need five pages of forms and three studies to consider a great idea.

Keep it Simple*

Strike three.

Get your hand off my knee.

You're overdrawn.

Your horse won.

Yes.

No.

You have the account.

Walk.

Don't walk.

Mother's dead.

Basic events require simple language.

Idiosyncratically euphemistic eccentricities are the promulgators of triturable obfuscation.

What did you do last night? Enter into a meaningful romantic involvement or fall in love?

What did you have for breakfast this morning? The upper part of a hog's hind leg with two oval bodies encased in a shell laid by a female bird or ham and eggs?

David Belasco, the great American theatrical producer, once said, "If you can't write your ideas on the back of my calling card, you don't have a clear idea."

How we perform as individuals will determine
how we perform as a nation.

By keeping the planning system simple, the technology of strategy planning is de-emphasized while the confrontation of strategic choices and the debate among the leadership from all levels is maximized. As the organization and its leaders develop, they can increase the sophistication of the strategy planning system. And they should.

* © United Technologies Corporation (1979), included with permission Harry Gray Associates.

Illustration. In a federal agency—the Department of Energy Exploration—the strategic planning process was designed originally to be simple and people driven. Required reading for all managers, the manual of procedures was a weighty document of almost forty pages. It included five to ten pages of forms on which departments and units could present their analyses and their strategic visions.

Unfortunately, the manual was read by very few people and the multi-year process sank under the weight of planning system complexity. None of the organization's members at various levels were willing to invest time and *study* to understand the complexities of the planning system. Instead, they chose to devote their time and energy—appropriately—to the creation of the organization's future, the real task of the planning process.

THE LESSONS OF PLANNING TECHNIQUES

Planners use various tools and techniques to respond to planning system design and process challenges. Many errors are made with the help of tools so there is much room for learning here. Some illustrative questions are as follows.

- How does the organization identify critical issues of strategic importance?
- How are critical competitors identified and categorized?
- How does the organization create a database to support the planning process?
- How are ideas and assessments from various stakeholders of the organization collected (including board members, executives, and employees)?
- What are the steps of the planning process?
- How does the planning include organization-wide participation?
- How do executives, managers, board members, and employees confront the difficult question of mission?

These questions are all of critical importance in designing and carrying out planning. Unfortunately, they also offer hard learned lessons on planning.

STEPS DEFINED

Lesson 37: The future goal was a fully renovated estate, but the plans for the access road were lost.

How do we engage in strategic planning? That is, what is the process used to guide the strategic planning work? Many commentators, academics, and executives have different labels for the steps in a strategic planning process. Some commentators have eight steps; others have three phases or an on-going cycle; while still others have pyramids with levels of work. An early writer, Steiner offered the following as a general process: (1) formulate the task, (2) develop inputs, (3) evaluate alternative courses of action, (4) define major objectives, (5) define major strategies and policies, (6) develop medium range details plans, (7) determine needed current decisions, (8) monitor performance, and (9) recycle annually. A model of the common elements of formal strategic planning systems appears in Appendix A.

It matters much less whether you call the flow of actions in the planning process a series of steps, phases, or part of a general planning cycle. What is important, however, is that the participants—executives, managers, and board members—have some clear sense of beginning, middle and end.

As noted in other lessons, planning is ongoing. However, there should be steps or phases that participants can understand as being the primary part of the planning period. For example, Ackoff's group has five phases called interactive planning: (1) formulation of the mess, (2) ends planning, (3) means planning, (4) resource planning, and (5) implementation and control.

The fundamental error often made is that the steps are not clearly presented, preventing the participants from understanding the flow of the process. Especially when the strategic planning work is new to the organization, the first iteration involves learning the process. In order to learn, participants must have a clear statement of what planning is. This lesson is often learned by confrontation, when participants ask quite directly "I'm not sure what we're doing." Or they ask—"What comes next?" If the planning designers and the executive in charge cannot answer directly a simple question about the process, then the steps are not clearly identified.

Ironically, the lack of a clear series of steps for the planning process is a mirror image of the error that planners are attempting to correct on an organizational level. Planners believe that an organization cannot get to its desired future unless there is a path for getting there. Yet they often attempt to run a planning process without a path.

A related part of this lesson concerns the complexities of the process. Some organizations make the mistake of inventing fourteen steps with three substeps, or five major stages with four phases in each and a series of steps in each of the phases. By the time planning participants are done understanding—or trying to understand—the phases, steps, and procedures, excitement is replaced by frustration. My own series of steps (published in a previous book) was purposely simplified to make them user friendly by synthesizing core elements of many models. Used in many processes over the years, my eight planning steps are:

Step 1 - Planning to plan
Step 2 - External analysis through environmental scanning
Step 3 - Internal Review through organizational systems analysis
Step 4 - Creative design or redesign of desired future
Step 5 - Matching the current and the desired future
Step 6 - Choosing strategies
Step 7 - Identifying actions and programs
Step 8 - Linkage to operation

We must keep in mind that the work is to be both intended/rational and emergent/intuitive within the steps. When it works well it is "crafted" and the whole of this strategic planning process can then be called strategy formation.

Illustration. In a 450 bed facility—Hill Medical Center—the planning process was described in a tree diagram. The diagram was divided into three or four sections, identified as levels. Each of the levels were to be accomplished as a part of the planning process. The participants—department managers, nurses, physicians and faculty members—were informed about the steps using the tree.

Despite its conceptually accurate form and representation of a solid planning process, the tree was overly complex. Reader after reader struggled to understand how each phase, step and level related to another. Who was to be involved at each point? What was the end point of the process? If these fundamental questions remain following the presentation of a graphic that purports to explain in single-page form the steps in the process, then all is lost.

Note(s)
Steiner, G.A. *Strategic Planning*. NY: Free Press 1979.

FOCUS GROUPS

Lesson 38: After identifying the stakeholders, we forgot to ask them for their vision of the future.

In another lesson we review the importance of *identifying* stakeholders, assessing their attitudes and values with regard to future scenarios (See Lesson 42). The planning challenge is how to collect information from the various stakeholders. Surveys and interviews are traditional tools.

While there are many techniques—personal interviewing, surveys, and town meeting-type sessions—few are quite as useful as a focus group for getting a rich, in-depth sense of a small group. Focus groups are relatively inexpensive and fairly easy to design and operate. However, the analysis of the information generated can be quite demanding as the comments are wide ranging.

Illustration. In the last several years, three organizations from very different industries have used focus groups to provide input to their strategic planning process. A banking association held nine focus groups state-wide to enable chief executive officers of their member banks to identify their needs and interests in the association's future.

A university hospital used focus groups to solicit the opinions of internal managers at all levels of the institution. Conducting six groups with some seventy managers, hospital executives were able to obtain strong involvement in the planning process and some new ideas for products and services.

Finally, one community interested in displaced workers held a series of focus groups with the workers themselves and with various corporate representatives to gain a sense of the problems and challenges presented to displaced workers. The focus groups sponsored by a labor management council were used in conjunction with community-wide surveys to support the creation of a stronger labor management future.

The lesson is that multiple methodologies—including focus groups—can be used to collect input from various stakeholders during the planning process.

PARTICIPATION DESIGNS

Lesson 39: Although we had the best intentions for participation, we were not successful because we lacked a design.

A lesson many executives learn is that they need to design participation into the planning process. One approach by Russell Ackoff offers a unique structure called the circular organization.

> The concept was originally developed to address a number of perceived needs: (1) to operationalize organizational democracy, (2) to increase the readiness, willingness, and ability to organizations to change, and (3) to improve the quality of working life. . . .
>
> The central idea in a circular organization is that every person in a position of authority—each manager and supervisor—is provided with a board. . . .
>
> At a minimum, the board at every level of the organization except at the top includes (1) the manager whose board it is, (2) his/her immediate superior, and (3) his/her immediate subordinates. . . .
>
> Boards normally have the following responsibilities: (1) planning for the unit whose board it is, (2) policymaking for the unit whose board it is, (3) coordinating the plans and policies of the next lower level, (4) integrating its own plans and policies and those of its immediately lower level with those made at higher levels, and (5) decision making regarding the quality of working life of those on the board.

Most of the strategic planning models call for broad participation but few have a design for doing so explicitly. The other important contribution of this model is that it begins to tie the strategic thinking to the daily decisions of operating managers in their boards. This truly represents a novel and more participative way to plan and to manage.

Illustration. Faced with problems of cost, quality and access, University Hospital is now using a circular design to address nursing and patient care problems. How does the hospital increase nursing recruitment and retention and simultaneously ensure quality of care? A planned approach is called for. The redesign process is driven by the circular design which creates a structure for participation in the planning process. The use of boards is a mechanism for expanding involvement, for co-designing the future and for generating management efficiency.

Note(s)
Ackoff, R.L. "The Circular Organization. An Update" *Acad. Mgmt. Executive.* 3; 1989; 11-16.

THREATS

Lesson 40: We were unaware that the hostile intentions and strong capabilities of competitors, along with the changing environment, threatened our well-being.

Once planners have looked inside at strengths and weaknesses, they need also to look outside the company. Depending on the planning sequence, planners can choose to look outside at external threats and opportunities *before* they examine internal strengths and weaknesses. Whichever order is chosen, threats are a key concern.

Orange County California found out that threats emerge with sudden and significant impact. The county treasurer invested heavily in financial derivatives and other volatile investments not counting on a major shift in interest rates—the situation beyond the county. The result was bankruptcy—a result most would see as strategic disaster.

There are several parts to this lesson. First, sometimes too many macro-level global threats are identified so that the group seems almost paralyzed by the listing. When a poor national economy or changing world affairs such as war in the Middle East override the discussion, the planners feel as if they've lost control of their organization's destiny. Overwhelming trends can push the planning group to a reactive "wait and see" mode, a dangerous position.

The second part of the lesson involves focusing the planning group's attention on the *key* threats, not the list of *all* possible threats.

While individual companies may be generally affected by changing regulations, by a national economy, by a new competitor, or by world affairs such as war, it is important that the planning group come to some consensus on the *key* threats most likely to have significant targeted impact. The national economy and climatic changes may be a concern but when a competing Fortune 500 company has "moved to town" that is probably the most significant and near-term threat to address.

Think about the threats from afar that have come to be very real. In a small town, Sherman's Shooters & Outfitters shop had no real competition for outerwear. In their rural area they were the only store. Then along came L.L. Bean.

Illustration. Several examples indicate the stunning changes that can be generated by the environment outside the boundary of the organization. In planning for one veteran's administration hospital, the planning group dutifully listed the threats that it thought it would be facing in the next several years.

The year was 2000.

In 2002 when they reviewed their list of threats, they were compelled to add a very significant one—war with Iraq. It had not appeared on the earlier list and would significantly affect the operations of the hospital in the next twelve months since they had responsibility for war casualties.

A second example comes from a very different organization, Waterford Landscape Service. The chairman of the board mentioned to his planners the need to continually monitor the weather. The planning group, all veterans of the landscape and nursery business, nodded in agreement.

With limited familiarity with the business, the planning consultant asked for a quick explanation.

The chairman remarked that it appeared that we were to enter a period of drought. While that drought may be short-lived, an extended one as in California had wreaked havoc on the state. Climate change is a definitive example of an environmental threat in the nursery business.

OPPORTUNITIES

Lesson 41: Our resources were strong and our competitors had stumbled, but we took no action because we saw no opportunities.

This lesson is derived from the purpose of the strategic planning process. Achieving a vision of the future requires a readiness to exploit opportunities that appear as the organization moves toward its vision.

BMW is a long standing maker of high quality luxury automobiles. When British Aerospace sold Britain's Rover Group to BMW, the BMW company moved closer to becoming a world class car company with a full range of products. Adding the Land Rover, an upscale vehicle, to the existing BMW line was at once a good complement to the existing product set and an opportunity for expansion.

Some executives, managers, and board members *expect* that opportunities will be presented to them. Other executives, board members, and employees feel that they need to search out and exploit the opportunities that always exist. Planners must see opportunity review as an intensive and ongoing hunt for new markets, for products or services, and for information on how to better meet the needs of future customers. As with threats, it is important for the planning group to clearly identify both broad areas and specific opportunities. Some executives even send their people to other countries to find new ideas as does the Chief Executive of Rubbermaid, a company legendary for its product invention and innovation.

Once opportunities are identified the task is to focus, as Herbold illustrates: "Microsoft has a lot of opportunities in front of it, and the company needs to be disciplined and focused to make them happen—to keep our eye on the big opportunities and not be deluded by marginal opportunities."

Illustration. One of the best illustrations of opportunities from the national environment is from the chairman of the National Nurserymen's Association. The planning design group was working on the schedule for a retreat for board members and staff. As the planning consultant reviewed the steps, discussing the point at which we would conduct the external review, the chairman stopped and asked what is "environmental scanning."

The consultant had forgotten that the terms *environmental* and *scanning* are jargon and have different meanings for executives in different fields. He explained that environment meant conditions and events outside the organization's boundaries and was more easily defined as "external." In effect, opportunities come from outside the business.

The Chairman replied "Oh, I've got a great one. Did you listen to the President's speech?"

Consultant: "What speech? Do you mean the other night?"

He said "Yes. The speech in which President Bush suggested that he would like to plant a billion trees."

Consultant: "Yes, I thought that was interesting and I like the environment, I think it's wonderful."

The Chairman replied: "No, you're missing it, when you're in the nursery business and the President of the United States wants to plant a billion trees, it's time to celebrate, it's opportunity!"

This clear example of an external opportunity tells us that the lesson is to identify the equivalent of planting a billion trees in your business.

STAKEHOLDER MAPPING

Lesson 42: We forgot to identify who is important to the organization's future.

Let's consider a recent example by a company long known for its attention to customers—the Walt Disney Company. Disney strategists decided to build a historical theme park near the Civil War battlefield at Manassas. They were not prepared for the strong opposition of historical groups, residents and leading newspapers. Deciding it was not worth the negative publicity and the long drawn out battle, they shelved their plans. Why were these vested interests not considered?

This lesson is about not paying attention—corrected by a technique called "stakeholder mapping." Many planning teams focus—mistakenly—on only the customers, employees and managers in "plain view." The stakeholder mapping theory calls this a failure of narrowness. An open search for persons connected to your business creates a much broader group as Mitroff notes:

Stakeholders are all those interest groups, parties, actors, claimants, and institutions—both internal and external to the corporation—that exert a hold on it. That is, stakeholders are all those parties who either affect or who are affected by a corporation's actions, behavior, and policies. Stakeholders typically compromise a much larger group than does the more limited class of claimants known as stockholders. The stockholders are only one of many competing and diverse groups that impact on the modern corporation, organization, or institution and must increasingly be considered by it if it is to survive, that is, if it is to assume control of its destiny.

The concept itself is simple. Stakeholder mapping involves a systematic search for persons inside and outside the organization that have some interest in the future well-being of the organization. As part of strategy formation participants identify all those persons with a stake in the organization's future. The list can begin with the obvious ones such as board members, executives, managers, and employees; but it should also include such stakeholders as suppliers, the consumers of services, government and regulating agencies, and community organizations that depend on the organization's philanthropy. The lesson learned as a result of stakeholder mapping is that there are typically far more stakeholders involved and interested in the organization's future strategies than originally thought.

Mapping generates knowledge of the values and positions of each of the stakeholder groups. What do clients and suppliers want from the organization? What do community organizations that depend on financial support need? Without information the new products or policies proposed by the organization in its drive toward its vision of the future may not fit stakeholder needs and may not generate support. Each of the stakeholders' positions are considered with regard to their degree of fit with the organization's vision of the future and its strategies for getting there.

Illustration. A community college with a very strong teaching and service record was beginning its planning process. Atlantic Community College served a small state capital community very well, providing education, training and continuing education services to members of public and private organizations. As the community college began to develop its vision of the future, it counted the state government as one of its major stakeholders. Many state agencies and public officials were located within blocks of the college.

Atlantic's planners correctly identified these stakeholders but could have gone further by expanding beyond employees of the agencies.

A stakeholder analysis with deeper exploration of state government interest would have indicated that a group of state legislators were very interested in creating a state capital-based four-year university. Some faculty and administrators felt this would stimulate competition for the community college. But to other faculty and some of the board members this was a real opportunity for the community college to create a very different future, a future as a four-year state-supported university.

The opportunity would have been identified more clearly and earlier with richer mapping, including systematic inspection of the positions and future interests of one stakeholder group, state legislators.

Note(s)
Mitroff, I.I. Stakeholders of the Organizational Mind. San Francisco, CA; Jossey Bass, 1983, p. 4.

BRAINSTORMING

Lesson 43: As if by magic, ideas should appear and be welcomed.

How does the planning team present and discuss new ideas and directions? Each planning process needs some mechanism by which new ideas "get on to the table." Nearly every manager is familiar with the phenomenon that occurs when a courageous person floats a new idea. The rest of the members of the group try to think of twenty reasons why the idea is silly, cannot work, could be too costly, or is not a good fit with their organization. By the time the critics are finished the original presenter of the idea is more inclined to have gone fishing than to help their organization think of new products or whole new directions.

United Technologies defined both problem and answer.

Oops[*]

An irate banker demanded that Alexander Graham Bell remove "that toy" from his office. That toy was the telephone.

A Hollywood producer scrawled a curt rejection note on a manuscript that became "Gone with the Wind."

Henry Ford's largest original investor sold all his stock in 1906.

Roebuck sold out to Sears for $25,000 in 1895. Today, Sears may sell $25,000 worth of goods in 16 seconds.

The next time somebody offers you an idea that leaves you cold, put it on the back burner.

It might warm up.

How we perform as individuals will determine how we perform as a nation.

Many organizations use brainstorming techniques that allow planners to offer ideas without evaluation or critique by their fellows. Most organizations make the mistake of not including enough brainstorming in the process. Leaders complain about the lack of creativity in the organizational culture; but they do not spend any time consciously attempting to surface ideas and ensure that the ideas have a fair hearing.

Brainstorming can be useful at each point of the planning process. For example, planners can brainstorm ideas about external

[*]© United Technologies Corporation (1981), included with permission of Harry Gray Associates.

threats and opportunities; they can brainstorm their analysis of internal strengths and weaknesses. And, they can brainstorm characteristics of alternative visions and innovative strategies that will move the organization into the future.

Most often, the error is not one of over-indulgence but of underutilization of the technique.

Illustration. In the Department of Human and Social Affairs brainstorming was not used. At first, the planning consultant thought that the planners did not see a need for this particular idea-generating process. Instead the consultant learned that agency leaders were more inclined to extend the past history of the agency into the future. For that kind of extension brainstorming was not really a useful process. To the contrary, brainstorming implies an openness to thinking about new ideas—any new ideas offered by participants. When they decided to try this technique they first faced discomfort and a lack of confidence in its ultimate usefulness.

ISSUES ANALYSIS

Lesson 44: There are hundreds of strategic issues, and we never said which three issues were key.

Critical "issues" frequently become the focus of strategy review during the years between major reviews of vision and mission. "Bubbling up" from almost anywhere, issues can include legislative, research and development, emergent competitors and communication problems. At Atlantic Richfield the responses require trend analyses, legislative reviews, position papers, testimony; all of which can flow into the strategy formation process.

The strategic planning process must identify and focus on a limited set of issues considered to be strategically important to the organization. Each day brings international and national changes from economic recessions to demographic changes in the population, to regional conflict, environmental catastrophe, and weather problems such as drought. These changes from "outside" must be considered by the organization as it plots its future.

Internal dynamics such as group conflict, the resignation of a key executive or the failure of a new business product also are strategically important to the organization's future. The potential number of issues to address is stunning. What must happen in the process is a careful winnowing of the long list of strategic threats and opportunities to a smaller number considered most important to be attacked at the present time.

A common problem is that the planners spend a good deal of time developing the list but relatively little time weeding out those of lesser importance. Although some groups have managed to sort the issues into top priority and secondary priority, many never endure the debate and conflict necessary to focus scarce analytical and response resources.

Illustration. For example, in American higher education there are many issues of importance to colleges and universities such as: the pressure to maintain educational leadership in emerging technologies; limited financial resources; expected faculty shortages; and students' demands for different kinds of education. All of these issues affect a college future. However, one—the demographics of eighteen year olds—may be of most critical strategic importance.

If Old Hickory College is relying on young full time students as its primary student base and the population of potential 18-year olds is shrinking, the planners must consider the strategic impact of this demographic shift. With the college dependent each year on a full class of freshmen for its financial operating margins, neglect of this concern is at the peril of survival. While other issues have importance as well—and should not be lost—the reduced pool of 18-year old students may be the most critical issue to be discussed at Old Hickory.

STRENGTHS

Lesson 45: Over the years, we knew we always did some things well, we just never looked to see which ones.

A strengths/weaknesses analysis is part of every planning process. The fundamental intent is quite straightforward. In order to be successful in the future, organizations must take the time to first identify and then build on their strengths. Executives should identify and eliminate their corporate weaknesses, since it is of little use to carry weaknesses into the organization's future.

For example, some organizations conduct an analysis of strengths only to find that it was their core business that they were good at. Sears examined the corporate contribution of their Allstate insurance, Dean Witter Reynolds brokerage and Coldwell Banker Real Estate finding that retail business was their strength and that they should focus on it. They eliminated the other businesses.

There are two parts to this lesson. First executives and managers rarely take the time to conduct a systematic strengths analysis. Since everyone in every department of every organization typically regards themselves as a strong contributor to their organization, the strengths analysis can be somewhat sensitive. The underlying assumption—silly when exposed—is that "organizations are good at everything," which is not true for any organization.

However, planners *must* come to agreement about which of the programs and units in the organization are the strongest. Without this agreement, we would suggest that new resources should be distributed equally through all of the units. Or, in times of cutback, all units of the organization should be forced to reduce resource use in equal amounts. Following this rule, the strong departments are penalized at the expense of the weak ones. This is not a good strategy.

A second part of the lesson—not often recognized—is that conducting a strengths analysis allows planning participants an opportunity to announce and celebrate.

> We do have an organization with strong components; here's what we've done well over the years....

Organizations pursuing excellence recognize that self-examination and celebration of success develop core values and boost morale. When the organization neglects this analysis, two messages are sent; (1) we have no strengths to announce; and (2) we are not interested in recognizing managers and employees for what they do well. Both are wrong.

Illustration. Leaders of a shelter, Housing Homeless, a nonprofit organization, had been pushing institutional development for seven years. Some major proposals were on the table including acquisition of land; radical expansion of programs and services; and the addition of several new buildings. All of the proposals fell short for various reasons ranging from financing to staffing.

During that year, a major donor presented a substantial sum of money to support the organization's endowment. In reviewing the year's accomplishments, the chief executive officer neglected to identify fund raising as a critical strength. There was no celebration of the good fortune or recognition of the strong organizational work that it represented. Most importantly, there was no attempt to understand the derivation of that fund raising strength. As the organization began to plan for its future, there were no data indicating how the endowment success was achieved and no information to help the organization build on that strength into its future. The strategic planning group wasted an opportunity and it ran a flawed incomplete process.

WEAKNESSES

Lesson 46: Like churchgoers before God, we struggle to find the courage to confront our failures.

The flipside of the internal strengths analysis is the identification of weaknesses. This part of the strategic planning process is also included in nearly all designs. Weakness analysis requires that planners confront a basic assumption that many executives, managers, employees and board members hold—namely that perfect organizations are possible. When we realize that no organization is perfect—because all human systems have flaws—then planners must move to confront the flaws and improve on their organization's structure and process in the future.

Consider the case of one well known transportation company—Greyhound. "How do you drive a leading company with a vaunted brand name to the brink of bankruptcy? Try mismanaging technology, misreading your market and alienating your shareholders. That was the losing formula followed by senior executives of Greyhound Lines until they finally lost their jobs in the latter half of 1994." A fouled up reservation system and failure to understand their key customers were leading problems. Without identification and confrontation of the flaws, there are no data to build a stronger organization in the future.

At its base, this lesson is an indicator of the level of maturity of the organization. Mature, open organizations are willing to identify and confront their weaknesses. Leaders are not cowed by the fact that they run imperfect organizations. They believe that a continued striving to do better is the model. Finding flaws is followed in lightning fashion with the expectation that they will be prevented where possible and corrected at every point.

Organizations conducting weakness analysis for the first time test the type of culture they have. An open culture enables and supports analysis of weaknesses. A closed culture (in which problems are never discussed but *buried*) requires extraordinary courage to offer even one sentence of criticism to seniors. Senior executives and middle managers can be open and supportive of a constructive dialogue about the weaknesses, or they an react defensively and attack bearers of the bad news.

How thorough is your examination of *your* company's weaknesses relative to existing or future competition? A different outcome may have resulted from recognition of the technical and market reception to the Beta VCR. One wonders whether cable television companies are paying adequate attention to the satellite dish companies—a combination of self-study of weakness and careful examination of new threats, our next lesson.

Illustration. In one of the earlier examples (see Lesson 19) a chief executive officer not knowledgeable about the nature of strengths-weaknesses analysis was horrified at the critical commentary by employees during the review of his company's weaknesses. He stopped the strategic planning retreat and sent everyone home. While this may be a far-end anxiety reaction to the strategic analysis of weaknesses, its variation is not uncommon.

Chief executives and board members that have seemingly understood that weakness analysis would be a part of the strategic review, cringe at the comments offered by employees and managers from various levels of the organization. But worse, they react defensively and/or respond with confrontation or criticism of the employees offering the analysis.

Needless to say, the employees and managers attempting to offer constructive criticism get the message—the bearer of bad news is bashed. Participants quickly learn that introspection and critical commentary are punished. And they also experience reinforcement of a core culture value—ignore and bury problems.

VISIONING

Lesson 47: A picture of the future was never painted; neither in the sharp detail of oil, nor the vague shadows of water colors.

Planning and strategy formation leads to a vision of the future. In the short-hand notation, vision is the destination that must be "seen" if strategy formation is considered complete. Hamel and Prahalad tell us why.

> Competitive innovation works on the premise that a successful competitor is likely to be wedded to a "recipe" for success. That's why the most effective weapon new competitors possess is probably a clean sheet of paper. And why an incumbent's greatest vulnerability is its belief in accepted practice.

Visioning is becoming increasingly popular even though we know too little about how to do it. Few organizations have actually bothered to *try* to create a vision of the future. Most often the vision presented as a result of the planning process is a careful extrapolation of the past. The *direction* of the future strategy is the past. Depending on the nature of the planning system design, the vision may be driven by financial analysis, a quantitative orientation and a narrow technological perspective of the organization.

In contrast, planners that paint a full picture address the vision in broad terms including: the nature of the products and services in the core business; why they are in the business; the structure of their organization; the expected quality of working life of executives, managers, and employees; management style and functions; the culture of their organization, the physical environment and how successes are celebrated. Consider this example of an announced vision presented by Mitsubishi Electric.

> To meet future challenges, Kitaoka has announced a sweeping agenda called "Vision 21." The goal, he says, is for Mitsubishi Electric to evolve into a "transnational enterprise" capable of accommodating the needs of fast-changing global society. "Politics tend to build national barriers," Kitaoka observes. "Even trade organizations tend to build regionally. But transnationals fly over frontiers."

Vision 21 targets six areas as being of paramount importance
to society: the environment, energy, health and fitness, leisure
amenities, security, and communication. A look at the company's
current operations shows that it is already active in fulfilling the
various objectives of Vision 21.

The *direction* is away from national to global with the "quick take"
on destination filled out by a set of indicators from operations.

A rich and full vision presents to the work force a picture that
can be captured and held; a sense of where they are moving to. In
some organizations it is a shared vision co-produced by executives,
managers, employees, and board. The creation may begin modestly
as Professor Ackoff suggests.

Design is a cumulative process. It is usually initiated by using
a very broad brush. Therefore, the first version is a rough sketch.
Then details are gradually added and revisions are made. The process continues until a sufficiently detailed design is obtained to enable others to carry it out as intended by its designers.

Some visions emerge in pieces often as a result of strong contact with customers. Microsoft acquired Intuit, sellers of popular
financial software. How does it fit their current vision? They are
not sure. But according to one commentator: "Microsoft believes
the seven million well educated users of Quicken, Intuit's personal
finance program will be in the vanguard of an army of electronic
consumers ready to shop, bank and invest via the evolving information infrastructure. Ready, that is, as soon as Microsoft sells them
the software they will need." The vision is consistent with what they
now do *and* it will expand based on evolving technology and opportunity.

Communicating and acting on the vision is an important follow-up step. Carol Kennedy reports that a Ciba-Geigy senior manager used a brief communique.

The details of how this vision was to be implemented were
then worked out in a "strategic direction plan", whose main objective was to give everyone in the organization a sense of identification with the company's goals, and a sense that those goals would
be compatible with their own ethics.

Thus, potential problems with "abstractness" and with disconnect to
the broader employee group were avoided by answering three ques-

tions. (1) If we will not replicate our past, what *direction* will we take—bigger, smaller, different? (2) When we arrive in the future, what will our organization be like (*destination*)? (3) What *decisions* will be needed to get us into the future?

The lesson is that exciting visions are made exciting by emergent thinking, by good images, and by a fullness that is not captured by a balance sheet. A vision of the future must reach beyond the bottom line to communicate in full detail the range of ideas and the enthusiasm and commitments of executives, managers, board members and employees.

Illustration. At the conclusion of the Consulting Engineering Group's planning meeting one of the senior planners—a board member—asked a simple and dry question—he thought.

"What will we be doing in the future that seems to be exciting?"

Rather than an avalanche of responses including a list of exciting strategies, programs, and actions, the room was silent.

The board member inadvertently but successfully surfaced the problem. The planning group had invested almost two days in planning and arrived at a vision of the future that was pretty much a reflection of their past. Very few new ideas had been proposed by the board members and executives. His comment both surfaced a flaw in planning and presented a challenge to the group. Produce creative ideas and an exciting vision or we all fall asleep or should go home, or both.

This was not the case at the Olde Colonial Candy Company. In their strategy sessions the CEO structured their search for a future by summarizing the debate with the d^3 questions; direction, destination and decisions. First he said, we want to go global and be larger, better able to compete with tough, successful companies like Hershey (*direction*). Second, in five years we want to be an international company with diversified product line, strong inroads into foreign markets and prominent name recognition outside the United States (*destination*). Third, we must make several key decisions: (1) whether to seek acquisition (companies with attractive products) or to greatly expand new product development; (2) which foreign joint venture partners to pursue; and (3) how we will restructure our US based organization (*decisions*). While far from complete, the strategy was beginning to emerge with vision and design as a cumulative process.

Note(s)

Linneman, R.E.; Klein, H.E. "Using Scenarios in Strategic Decision Making." *Business Horizons* 28, no. 1 (1985): 64-74.

Ackoff, R.L. *Creating the Corporate Future.* New York: Wiley, 1981, p. 113-114.

Wilson, I. "Realizing the Power of Strategic Vision." *Long Range Planning* 25(5); 1992.

Aughton, P. "Participative Design within a Strategic Context" *J. Quality and Participation.* March 1996; 68-75.

Hamal, G.; Prahalad, C.K. "Strategic Intent." *Harvard Bus. Rev.* May-June 1989, p. 71.

Kennedy, C. "Changing the Company Culture at Ciba-Geigy" *Long Range Planning* 26(1); 1993; p. 19.

Stewart, J.M. "Future State Visioning Technique at National Rubber Company" *Planning Review.* Mar-Apr 1994; 20-33.

THE MISSION SWAMP

Lesson 48: Without a definition driven by data, the organization's mission oozed everywhere—like a swamp.

One of the most critical parts of the strategy planning process is the creation or redesign of mission. For new organizations or subunits the question is what should the mission be? For existing organizations the question is does the old mission remain viable or, should it be adapted to better suit the organization's future purposes, products and services?

The old mission may be quite appropriate but some change is needed to address new customer requirements and environmental pressures. The defense industry provided an example when two producers of defense products—fighter planes, missiles and satellites—Lockheed and Martin Marietta decided to merge to become one very large and very capable defense contractor. There was no mission change here but a large leap deeper into the traditional purpose of each company.

The technical planning problem here is when and how to confront the question of mission. The lesson that organizations often learn is that when missions are confronted first, there is little use to the outcome of interminable discussion.

Some planners begin with a presentation of mission at or near the start of the process as in the following John Bryson model.

1. Initiate and agree upon a strategic planning process.
2. Identify organizational mandates.
3. Clarify organizational mission and values.
4. Assessing the organization's external and internal environments to identify strengths, weaknesses, opportunities, and threats.
5. Identify the strategic issues facing the organization.
6. Formulate strategies to manage these issues.
7. Review and adopt the strategic plan or plans.
8. Establish an effective organizational vision.
9. Develop an effective implementation process.
10. Reassess strategies and the strategic planning process.

The fundamental error shows up almost immediately. The planning participants struggle mightily with questions of philosophy and intent; the nature of the business; the distribution system of products and services; core goals and values; and how the organization will be different in the future. These questions are all relevant when exploring mission, but by addressing mission in Step 3 as Bryson does, or by starting with mission, there is no database for examining the various elements of the mission statement.

Conversely, when the mission statement is examined well into the strategic planning process, the database has been established with which to evaluate a proposed and/or a revised mission statement. Planners use the external analysis, the internal strengths/weaknesses review and the newly developed vision. How can planners answer questions of mission without a vision of the future which must be created first? Mission should include points about why we exist, core competencies, markets, customers and clients, economic objectives and core values.

In my own process, for example, the planning work *before* the mission review includes an external analysis, an internal examination of strengths and needs and creation of a vision of the future. At this point in the process, the mission review incorporates data about threats and opportunities, desired directions and destination.

In similar fashion, Ackoff's planning model proposes creation and review of the mission *after* the formulation of scenarios about the present. These scenarios—he calls them "mess formulation,"—include external reviews of environmental changes, internal analyses and stakeholder mapping. Once the design for the organization's

future is created, the mission is matched to that design and the previous analyses of threats, opportunities, strengths and weaknesses.

When missions are analyzed and created first, they tend to be
broad enough to cover all the interests of the participants and a wide
range of potential customers. However, the interests of participants
and the undefined needs of customers are typically so great that the
organization's definition is not bounded, but instead seems to flow
all over like a swamp.

Illustration. The lesson regarding mission is best illustrated by a
prominent west coast university. The Dean decided that a statement
of mission was an important beginning point as he knew from the
literature on planning that it was a key component. As the college
planners worked through their mission statement, they proposed
that their core interests were *teaching, research, and community
service.*

However, as they moved into the mission discussion, questions
arose regarding what kinds of research would dominate the future:
basic or applied research and, for example, what kinds of service
would be most appropriate? Service to which parts of the community would be stressed -the corporate community, the federal government community, or the voluntary non-profit sector? Because the
debate rapidly rose to a high level of conflict, the planners decided
to let stand some broad statements about the toleration of a wide
range of teaching interests, research interests from basic to applied,
and service to the total community. While this successfully resolved
the conflict within the planning group, it did nothing whatsoever to
focus the mission of the organization.

A careful inspection of the university's actual operations would
show that teaching was very specifically targeted to elite students,
that research was applied in nature and that much of the service
work was directed at the federal government community. By first
stating and underscoring these interests based on external competitors, the needs of critical stakeholders, internal reviews of education
and research work currently performed (strengths/weaknesses), the
planning group could define a more specific sense of mission for the
future.

Note(s)
Bryson, J.M. *Strategic Planning for Public and Non-Profit Organizations.* (3rd Edition).
  San Francisco, CA: Jossey Bass, 2004.

SCENARIOS AT WORK

Lesson 49: Scenarios are for thought, not for prediction.

One of the challenges in strategic planning work is how to stimulate discussion of alternative futures. Many organizations have rich histories of tradition complete with successful policies and practices, quality products and well received service. But the world does change. Consider for a moment the plight of camera shops that have not developed expertise in processing digital photos. One useful way to imagine alternative futures is to use scenarios. While scenarios are, to some extent, a compilation of external and internal reviews, an integrated scenario ties many trends, issues, threats, opportunities, strengths and weakness together into a coherent whole. The best scenarios provide a provocative and unexpected view of the future. They are best used for generating dialogue and debate, not for prediction (as Mintzberg has noted)—there are far too many possible scenarios. Trying to predict the future through the use of scenarios is very much like the lottery—the planning team has a slim chance of hitting the mark.

Illustration. One association learned the prediction lesson quite well. The Rocky Mountain Banking Association had served the state's banking institutions for 102 years. Their annual planning exercises (including a scenario) called for more of the same services to members: education, policy analysis, legislative lobbying, and management support. As the sole banking association in the state, they felt basically secure in their future of continuing service to their 245 members. Large banks comprised about 25% of the member institutions. Large bank members who were acutely aware of the national trends toward economies of size wanted to encourage consolidation – smaller community banks would be acquired (either by friendly or hostile means). Association leaders were caught in the middle as smaller community banks wanted to actively resist this new direction. Since large banks paid the largest share of the dues, their pro-consolidation stand won out. The scenario for the future – continuing on as usual – turned out to be a wrong prediction. Some 140 small banks joined to form a competing banking association, ending the solidarity that had lasted for 102 years (and demonstrating that unexpected futures can emerge).

LESSONS OF STRATEGIES AND PROGRAMS

In this group of lessons we address problems of strategy and program planning. Planners often fail to link the vision of the future with the detailed operational programming necessary to insure that the future actually comes about.

There are seven lessons in this section addressing these topics:

- understanding strategy
- making choices
- program planning
- budgeting
- responsibility assignments
- resource acquisition
- changes to the plan

These lessons help to ensure a linkage between the abstract, conceptual work of vision and mission and the day-to-day responsibilities of managers and employees "in-the-trenches."

This section and the final part of this book, Lessons in Progress, Outcomes and Benefits ensure that planning is not just an interesting intellectual exercise but one that has real payoffs for the organization in terms of actions and accomplishments.

STRATEGY

Lesson 50: We all agreed that we had a strategy for the future; but when asked to identify it, none of us could do so.

All organizations have strategies—some are openly defined while others are covertly practiced. Strategies are patterns of behavior—ways of acting and deciding that help to form a path to the future. Strategic planning is a force for pushing strategy to the forefront of corporate consciousness linking *direction, destination* and *decisions.*

Strategy can be equivalent to and inclusive of strategic planning but Tregoe and Tobia think that often they are not. In their view planning does *not* produce strategy because it is based on projections; is too prediction and finance oriented; comes up from the bottom levels to be aggregated; rests on untested assumptions; is inflexible and short range. Strategic planning can produce strategy but only after addressing these deficiencies.

However, long before the language and the popularity of strategy, entrepreneurs and managers at all levels in public and private organizations had it. Some "announce" their strategy as does Microsoft with a series of actions that reveal decisions and some direction, if not a full destination.

> So here we are at the beginning of 1995. Gates' team has professionalized its sales force, redoubled its market research efforts, realigned product development efforts, dodged serious sanctions from the Justice Department, and tightly focused its researchers on real problems. What's next?

This lesson is about surfacing, evaluating and adapting the strategy the organization has been pursuing, or will pursue.

Let's consider an example in the education field. We can ask is the university striving to be larger in size, no matter what the expense? Do the board and the deans seek more and more students, more research clients and more buildings? If so, *growth*—to become bigger in size—is the driving strategy that pushes the school into the future. However, if the future of the university is best arrived at by paying careful attention to financial concerns, or by developing current academic degrees, then growth is not the strategy.

It is difficult to propose new strategies without consciously identifying and examining the strategy now employed. The process of identifying and reviewing strategy assists planners in learning how it has succeeded with its past endeavors. Strategy review tests the degree of fit between the existing strategy and a changing organizational environment. Strategies—like changes in the external world and the internal organization—also change.

Illustration. Some years ago, as health care cost containment concerns were just emerging, Greater Washington Hospital reorganized itself as a holding company. The holding company concept was used to manage the cost containment pressures while simultaneously opening new opportunities in related areas of business. A diversified health care company with subsidiaries in hotel, food and physician practices was the vision.

Unfortunately, the strategy of development was not clearly proposed in open fashion where it could be critically examined by all the parties. As a result, the holding company concept became a green light for the pursuit of any new product or service idea. Five or six years into the development of the new organizational structure, managers and employees began screaming. It seemed to them that the hospital—or what was once the hospital—was now in wild pursuit of products and services in any direction the proposer desired (unrelated to health care).

In effect, the strategy that was thought to be driving the holding company was causing internal disorganization and lack of focus. But it was not until the strategy was surfaced and critically examined that executives and managers understood that a new direction had been unconsciously stimulated by the redesign of the organization.

Note(s)
Tregoe, B.; Tobia, P.M. "Strategy Versus Planning: Bridging the Gap" *Journal of Business Strategy*. 1991, pp. 14-19.

RATIONALISTS ARE MAPPING

Lesson 51: Maps display interstate routes because they run in straight lines and provide the shortest distance from A to B.

Correlating mapping with the strategy process is a risky endeavor. The criticism of Henry Mintzberg—that strategic planning has suffered from an excess of rationality—comes to mind. If we could only achieve strategy success as easily as we find our way with a map, we would indeed be able to run many more high performance organizations. But events, people and so-called irrational behaviors intrude. Intuitive–emergent strategies are often not on a map – they are missed by "conscious rational analysis." We miss them as we would an interesting inn or a small unknown restaurant.

Illustration. The Bureau of Citizen Services (BCS) is a state agency in the Mid-Atlantic region. Aware that federal agencies were required to create strategic plans, the Governor ordered all agencies in his state to create plans as well. BCS administrators began crafting what they thought was to be a detailed "map" for getting to the future. As the planners proceeded, they became bogged down in the multiple details of what they had always thought was operational planning. As with contracts, they established timelines for various milestones, complete with deliverables and resource requirements. The 240 page volume was called "Map to the Future" and was widely distributed. Literally months after they circulated the report, politics, restructuring and economic changes interrupted their carefully constructed route. Planners creating a "map" did not have the capacity to adapt, fearing that they could not deviate from the plan lest they "get lost."

STRATEGIC CHOICES

Lesson 52: Faced with hard choices, we made none.

As they move through the planning process executives, managers and board members generate new ideas for products and services. However, quite often those planners *most* successful at generating new ideas are the *least* successful at deleting already existing products and services. With a wealth of financial and human resources, new ideas can be accommodated, along with maintenance of existing ones. But increasingly both public and private organizations are being called on to make choices; to give up some products and services when they choose to develop new ones.

A concise presentation of the lesson of strategic choices adapted from Below and colleagues uses three questions:

- Which of our businesses, products, and services shall we *maintain* in our future?
- Which of our businesses, products, and services will we *add* in the future?
- Which of our businesses, products, and services will we *delete* from our organization's future?

It is the final question that causes most strategists the most difficulty. Because all individual products and services and whole lines of business have a champion, there is terrific personal investment to overcome.

But if the planners decide that they will maintain all current products and services in the future, they deny the dynamic environment—changes in customer needs and desires. Additionally, new lines of business strain existing resources and eliminate the ability to focus attention on ones that will be winners for the organization.

To maintain all existing products and services, to add some and to delete none, means that the organization is running a perfectly balanced system, with all areas contributing at the A-plus level. While this is theoretically possible, I have yet to identify one company as an example.

Illustration. The Recreational Facilities Association was engaged in a planning process that required them to review six major program areas. With a small staff of under ten persons, the planning process was approached sensitively so that no one was offended by the review. Both board and staff planners were careful to support leaders of the various programs, including education, membership, legislative affairs and technical services.

At the start, both board members and staff eagerly threw out new ideas for products and services. This dynamic group had seemingly no shortfall of suggestions. Each of the programs was reviewed with one to three new initiatives added in each area.

As the planners worked their way through the process, the facilitator suggested that it was time to search for items to delete. The group, somewhat shocked, became silent. In their view, the purpose of planning was to add new products and services. The question of deleting never really entered their minds and in fact was discomforting. The process ended with the group not able to identify any products or services for elimination.

Unfortunately, the lesson learned was that since the budget was not increasing, there were no resources to pursue any of the ideas. Freeing resources by dropping programs was not a decision option.

COLLABORATION AND COMPETITION

Lesson 53: Some partnerships create a strategic paradox, requiring collaboration and competition.

We usually think of strategy as a neat and clean statement that narrows ambiguity. Many of us, however, face the paradox that we need to collaborate with our competitors. Both private and public industries are engaged in numerous joint ventures to create or market products and services. For example, universities have long joined together in research partnerships with other research universities; hospitals jointly create and operate regional laboratory services; defense industry companies often bid on projects as a team. These strategies require technology sharing, building a climate of trust and teamwork, structuring of shared incentives, and mediating the culture which sees the competitor as "the enemy." While collaboration can be extremely difficult to engineer, the results are found in expanded capacity, broader markets, and the development of new skills.

Illustration: Doctors Medical Group (DMG) is a large multi-specialty firm with 75 physicians and over 200 support staff. The cardiovascular physicians have watched their field advance rapidly over the past 20 years. New interventions and new drugs enabled solid progress in the management of heart disease and related disorders. As they lobbied their favorite hospitals for new technologies and staff, they found capital for expansion and a willingness to "stretch" absent. Since the physicians were organized as a separate group, joined to the hospital by contract, they began to see a free standing heart facility as their future. Creating a free standing facility would place them in competition with the hospital and, as the hospital depended on cardiac revenues, the competition would escalate quickly to conflict. Through a six-month series of negotiations, DMG was able to fashion a joint venture that included co-ownership of a new wing of the hospital, now designated as a Heart Institute. During negotiations, physicians and hospital administrators had to learn to collaborate with their competitors, simultaneously looking out for their own interests and the interests of the partnership.

PROGRAMS

Lesson 54: At the 1990 meeting, programs created in the eighteenth century were retained by silent affirmation—but the visitor objected.

When we create a new vision of the organization's future, we can expect program changes. Sometimes the program changes are literally changes in "programming" as at the Public Broadcasting Service. PBS is facing pressure to change both its vision of the future and day-to-day programming.

> Big Bird, meet Mrs. Frizzle and Bill Nye the Science Guy. A quarter of a century after introducing the nation's preschoolers to the rainbow-colored puppet cast of "Sesame Street," the Public Broadcasting Service is dramatically expanding its educational TV family—and recasting itself in a new role. In a move that turns nine hours of PBS's daytime schedule over to children's programming, the nonprofit network this week is launching PTV, the Ready to Learn Service on PBS. The new lineup combines old standbys like "Sesame Street" and "Barney" with four new shows emphasizing science, reading and multiculturalism.
>
> While no doubt good news for education-minded parents, PBS's creation of PTV is also a calculated attempt to establish a niche for itself in an increasingly competitive television industry. With the explosion of cable channels, video and other media aimed at kids, and with the recent grumbling about whether public television is worth taxpayers' dollars, PBS is struggling to clarify its role on the airwaves. "The question is, 'What is unique about PBS in a world of 50 or 500 channels?'" says PBS's new president, Ervin Duggan.

Changing the role of the PBS has implications for daily television offerings. Changing them will be difficult for leaders and employees.

This lesson is a subtle follow-up to the strategic choices question; what businesses, products, and services we maintain should be a debate, not an automatic stamp of approval. As we begin to consider actions to follow the planning, the question does involve what programs should be added, deleted or maintained as noted in Lesson 49. With no one to assist the process, the group takes the easy path, no products or services are dropped. The "traditional" programs are maintained in deference often to the founders and the founders' vision. This is one point where an outside facilitator is helpful. The facilitator's role is to establish a trusting, supportive climate in which the exploration of program options (including deletion) can be comfortably but fully discussed. As anxieties over program termination rise, the importance of an outside referee is especially important.

Illustration. Because *all* research is important, scientists are often at their worst in this part of the process. At National Research Lab, a research and development subsidiary of an international company, senior scientists were informed that if they could identify department level programs that they would consider deleting, new resources would be directed at department needs they felt were appropriate. One group in particular spent many afternoons discussing the merits of a program in AIDS research. It seemed that two promising directions did not work out and a senior project scientist left to join a university. After much soul-searching and hard debate, they voted as a group to delete a program offered by members of their research team sitting in the room. As a result of this decision, the lab fully supported the redirection of scientists' resources to a proposed new cancer drug. The strategic decisions made by the scientists and follow-up support reinforced the targeted use of scarce resources and demonstrated the effectiveness of the strategic planning process.

Note(s) ·
Toch, T. "Public Television Feathers its Nest" *U.S. News & World Report.* July 18, 1994; 52-53.

FINANCES

Lesson 55: At last we came to finances. Some planners were grumpy, thinking that this part of the process should have been the *whole* process.

One of the most difficult lessons to learn in strategic planning is the balance required in addressing finances. Executives and managers from the finance department often insist that this is both the beginning and the ending point of the whole strategic process. At the very first meeting, they identify the constraining financial factors that should drive (and limit) the options. This is a terrible trap, as it undercuts broader vision and limits the creative possibilities, and it can do damage.

The financial support for new strategy involves both owner/executives and producer-employees. Focusing on the money can lead to a neglect of the image and standing of the product. Consider the case of baseball. In 1994 owners and players were perceived by their national customers as greedy. But they were attending to money as the key aspect of their vision of the baseball future. The conflict produced not just a strike but a tarnished perspective on a national pastime that may have significant financial implications for the teams.

At the close of the planning process there is an equally dangerous point related to financial interests and reactions. After much enthusiasm regarding new planning options and possible program directions, inevitably someone remarks:

"But there isn't financial support for any of this; therefore we can do nothing."

Or worse than that, financial officers state, "We should do nothing until the financial clouds are cleared."

These comments direct the group to a no-action response that effectively dampens the whole process by citing lack of financial capability and heightening uncertainty.

The true "bottom line" is careful attention to the financial side but in a way that does not allow the financial perspective to inhibit interest in the future. Organizations can clear incredibly high financial barriers with creativity and innovation when the group is committed to an exciting vision.

Illustration. One of my first experiences in planning involved a fourteen month-long process. During this fourteen month period I learned the financial lesson.

The chief financial officer began the very first meeting by monopolizing the floor to repeatedly ask why planning was important when the financial situation was so uncertain. No budget for development existed he said. At every meeting through the fourteen months he continued to raise the importance of the financial direction of the organization and how the limited finances should constrain options. Although the planners attempted to persuade him that finances can be handled, he refused to hear the message. New products were proposed and successfully funded but always with much energy expended to overcome financial objections.

At the final meeting of the planning group, the chief financial officer ended his involvement in the planning process where he began, by stating vociferously the limits imposed by finances. He was not successful in killing the process but he presented a formidable barrier through his lack of understanding.

BUDGET

Lesson 56: The budget was completed before the planning process, and it was never amended.

One place to look for strategy formation impact is in the budget. Budget limitations can be used to drive the planning process as attempted by the chief financial officer in Lesson 55. What is not in the budget cannot be enacted. The converse is also true.

When planners do not take care to ensure that the budget reflects changes in resource directions and priorities, then the budget will not
distribute resources needed to move forward. If the budget does not change, the future will be very much like the past.

The lesson involves two types of errors:

- The budget drives the planning process from start to finish, constraining ideas and dampening enthusiasm.
- The budget has no relationship to the desired future, and thus does not support movement toward the future.

The budget cannot be allowed to limit vision and it ultimately must be used to map resource distribution for changes in the company.

Illustration. At River Region Community Services, the timing of planning and budgeting seemed to be disconnected. When planning was conducted early in the year it was reflected in the budget prepared for the next calendar year. But participants at the budgeting session (late in the fall) often felt reduced enthusiasm for the new visions and directions that were created in the previous fall and at the beginning of the calendar year.

Recognizing this problem, the organization tried to move the planning process closer to the budgeting period. However, as the planning process began to overlap with budget negotiations, it seemed that there was not quite enough time to finish the planning prior to the initiation of the budget work. When the overlap occurred, budgeting considerations seemed to take precedence over vision and program ideas, with the budget again driving the planning.

RESPONSIBILITIES

Lesson 57: When the plan was completed we ran around in circles; no one knew who should do what first.

One test of the viability of visionary ideas is to ask for volunteers to take on different tasks. If few step forward, the vision of the future is tacitly questioned.

This lesson is directed at the careful assignment of responsibilities for carrying out results of the planning (such as new policies and feasibility or marketing studies). Each action required to attain the future must have staff responsibility, otherwise progress stalls. One formal process is called responsibility charting (Galbraith). Formalizing the process can succeed because it presses staff to pick up some piece of this work.

Future building tasks must be built into the reward structure. The future then begins to appear piece-by-piece as staff-assigned responsibilities are accomplished.

The lesson is acutely learned when the planning group reviews progress at six month or yearly intervals. When it becomes clear that there are overlapping responsibilities with no focused assignments, the lack of progress is apparent.

Illustration. At the Mid Atlantic Economic Development Corporation (MAEDC), the vision of the future called for closer linkages between the corporate and state government communities. One of the methodologies proposed was advisory groups.

Two levels of advisory groups were to be created, one organization-wide, the second industry-by-industry groups (e.g. manufacturing, transportation, retail, health). The first advisory group was initiated and began functioning within a year after the proposal was suggested. However, some two years after the original proposal, industry groups still had not established their boards.

When chief executives were questioned about why this had not occurred, they suggested that they assumed it was the responsibility of the MAEDC chief executive to create an advisory group nomination process. When the MAEDC chief executive was asked why this did not happen, he said he felt that advisory groups should be an autonomous responsibility of the industry groups. Although, he did suggest that he might like to be involved in selecting the members. Obviously, the responsibility assignment for one aspect of the organization's future—building relationships through advisory groups—was not very clear. As a result, neither group acted—a piece of the future did not emerge.

RESOURCES

Lesson 58: "There are no resources! Absolutely none!" cried the pessimists. But we were so excited about the future we forced ourselves forward.

In case after case, a major barrier seems to be the lack of resources to enact the new strategy. Pessimistic members insist that resources are stretched thin; that there is no possibility of adding new business lines or even individual products or services.

First, the lesson involves relearning an assumption: resources must be found within the existing resource set. I believe strategy formation is most effective when it confronts the existing allocation of resources and results in resource shift. Without redistribution, maintenance of current resource levels implies support for all ongoing activities—which supposedly were to change as a result of strategic analysis.

Second, this lesson suggests that when people in organizations want to do something badly enough, they find the resources to make it happen. This is a well known characteristic of entrepreneurial organizations. Chronically short of start-up monies, of maintenance monies, of "go-ahead" monies, entrepreneurs become inventive, creating new flows of cash, facilities and personnel that were nonexistent at the first proposal of the idea.

For example, Southwest Airlines is a low cost, high service company recognized for its innovation. But its new products, services and support systems are based on a key resource according to Henkoff: "The hardest thing for rivals to copy seems to be [CEO] Kelleher's secret weapon—the trust and respect of his employees." What a strategic weapon.

When pessimists rule, both enthusiasm and creativity are dampened. Many resource problems have been solved by linking creativity with commitment to an alternative future. Russell Ackoff's comment is relevant: "The principal obstruction between us and the future we most desire is ourselves."

Illustration. At Brandon University some years ago, computer resources were too limited to support the future the department's faculty had in mind—a department with active computer use by students and faculty. It was suggested that faculty apply to the university's central office for equipment and support. At that time, resources were stretched thin. The response from central office was no money for computers for several years.

Departmental faculty took the position that computers were an integral part of faculty work and could not be done without. In discussions about the problem faculty remembered that project monies are committed to a general fund that can be used for professional and institutional development. Several faculty agreed to commit their project salary savings to the purchase of departmental computers.

Pessimists had suggested that there was nothing to do but wait until the central office delivered the computers. But a vision of the future—a department with computer support—became reality by individual faculty members engaging in project activities that produced the resources.

UNEXPECTED EXTERNALS

Lesson 59: Thinking we could foresee everything, the call for trees and the call for war proved us wrong.

The history of strategic planning systems development over the last several decades has been written by academics. One phase was called "predict and prepare." Planning was designed to enable executives, managers and board members to predict the future and prepare their organization to take advantage of it. Unfortunately, prediction is an inexact science and will never remove unexpected externals from the situation. The "predict and prepare" school of planning is dead.

Previous illustrations offered two strong examples of this lesson. Despite good comprehensive planning systems, a veterans administration hospital and a nurserymen's association were unprepared for external surprises. In its planning work from 1987 to 1989, the veterans administration hospital did not consider the possibility of war. War in the Middle East meant the V.A. hospital would assume responsibility for handling casualties, an unexpected external event that dramatically affected 1990-91 plans.

The nurserymen's association had an unexpected and much more pleasant opportunity arise. In general the greening of America has led to a greatly increased concern for the environment. The first President George Bush's call to plant a billion trees was an unexpected external "surprise" that provided nurserymen with opportunities nationwide. Neither war nor the call for trees was expected.

The future cannot be predicted but we do need to pay attention. The lesson is that in planning for uncertainty, unexpected external situations will always be present. Some will emerge as wonderful opportunities while others will be threats—both must be successfully managed in order to ensure a future.

Illustration. One state college system urgently in need of capital expenditures to support existing student levels was shocked to find its state government in dire budget straits. Planning predicted capital improvements would move forward aggressively under a governor with a strong education agenda. But revenue shortfalls and budget expenditures way over revenues created a classic threat—an unexpected external in the first year. Dramatic budget cutbacks appeared at the start of the new administration. Although the problem was to be corrected in future years it was a totally unexpected threat that the organization experienced and could not predict.

Bank One, a large regional bank, was extremely successful in the 1980s. But the next fifteen years brought stiff external competition and began to make significant inroads into deposits, profit margins and future potential. The "externals" included legislative and regulatory prohibitions against selling mutual funds and insurance. A whole group of very strong competitors emerged—non-banks including mutual funds and stockbrokers, automobile finance companies, mortgage and credit card companies. Banks felt both the characteristics of the external environment (regulatory constraints) and active competitors *external* to their prime industry—banking.

CASES

CASE 11: FIRST TRINITY EVANGELICAL LUTHERAN CHURCH

Religions and their institutional member churches also face strategic questions. Church boards struggle with the same types of issues related to budgets, program priorities, and memberships. The First Trinity Evangelical-Lutheran Congregation of Pittsburgh was organized on January 22, 1837. Led by The Reverend "Father" Heyr, the first services were held in a Unitarian meeting house on Smithfield Street in downtown Pittsburgh. In 1840, the first Evangelical-Lutheran church building was constructed. The congregation later moved to Oakland, a suburb of Pittsburgh. Construction of the present Trinity Church began in 1926 with completion and dedication in 1927. Corbusier and Lenski, famed architects from Cleveland, designed the church in the fifteenth century Gothic style.

In discussing the future, Trinity Lutheran addressed some of the issues facing churches across America, including: the aging of the membership, how to recruit and retain younger members, the relative importance of social versus religious causes, competition for donations, and the prioritization of local versus national and international causes. Upkeep of the facilities and linkage with the greater community are always important as well.

Trinity Lutheran Church offers fellowships to students of the University of Pittsburgh, Carnegie-Mellon, Chatham College, Duquesne University, and other colleges. The fellowship is committed to helping students grow and mature in the Christian faith through the teachings of the Lutheran Church–Missouri Synod. It also offers classes for international students who have English as a second language (ESL).

In every community, churches involve their members in discussions of topics of interest to local citizens and their collective future. Many church members serve on various committees and boards.

Website: http://www.firsttrinity.net/

Questions: What are the strategic issues facing each individual church and how do these issues interact with concerns about the greater growth of the denomination and religion in general?

Case 12: PENNSYLVANIA CAPITOL POLICE FORCE

Community and special group policing is an integral part of our modern society. Each policing organization must think about its mission, values and operational future. The Pennsylvania Capitol Police Force was established in 1895 as the first Pennsylvania police agency under Commonwealth jurisdiction and the second oldest state police organization in the United States. The original force was made up of six members who had the authority to protect state property and to enforce order on state grounds and in state buildings. Since the Capitol Police was first established in 1895, its responsibility has grown. Today it is charged with achieving a safe environment, investigating all crimes committed on state property, protecting employees and visitors while on state property, and protecting property and grounds throughout the Capitol Complex and at state office buildings in Philadelphia, Pittsburgh and Scranton. These services are accomplished by bicycle patrol, foot patrol, K-9 patrol, or police vehicle patrol. The Capitol Police maintains a constant (24 hours a day, seven days a week) presence in Harrisburg and Philadelphia.

Website: http://www.dgs.state.pa.us/

Questions: How does the Capitol Police force relate to community police organizations and to the greater state police? How does it address new strategic issues such as security for government officials and citizens?

Case 13: STATE MUSEUM OF PENNSYLVANIA

Museums across the country are addressing the need to update old exhibits. Pennsylvania's museum is no different. Located in the state capital of Harrisburg, The State Museum of Pennsylvania covers all aspects of Pennsylvania history and holds significant collections. The State Museum hosts more than 315,000 school children and adult visitors annually. It offers a variety of learning opportunities and resources. Educational programs are designed to encourage visitors to explore and experience the stories of Pennsylvania's past.

Programs vary from the Planetarium, where astronomy and the latest discoveries in space science are explained through multi-media, to discovering Coelophysis bones in the Dino Lab. The State Museum Planetarium has just introduced a new concept in Planetarium projection called the digital planetarium. The Museum is working with the Capital Area Intermediate Unit to provide professional development opportunities to upper elementary and middle school teachers. Through a combination of visits and online coursework, the program will use the Museum's zoological and botanical collections and staff expertise to share current knowledge with teachers. Recently the Museum opened Curiosity Connection, a kid-inspired "world of wonder" where families with children ages seven and younger can discover, learn and play together.

Website: http://www.statemuseumpa.org/home.html

Question: What are the strategic issues for museum managers, especially public operations? How can museums be made more interesting? And how could museums collaborate with each other to build visitors and recognition of their value?

CASE 14: SOUTHWEST AIRLINES

Airline transportation has grown significantly over many decades, but has become a troubled industry. More than 34 years ago, Rollin King and Herb Kelleher founded a different kind of airline for passengers, created to provide high quality services at low cost. Started as a small Texas airline, Southwest (SW) Airlines flies more than 70 million passengers a year to 60 cities all across the country (3,000 flights a day).

Southwest has 436 of the newest jets in the nation, with an average age of 9 years. They are the first airline with a frequent flyer program to give credit for the number of trips taken and not the number of miles flown. They also pioneered senior discounts, Fun Fares, Fun Packs, same-day airfreight delivery service and ticketless travel. Any SW flier can get a discount on rental cars, cruises, hotels, vacation packages and tickets to theme parks like Disney World,

Orlando Sea World, Busch Gardens, etc. SW consumers can save money at movie links and FTD (sending fresh flowers and gifts) and obtain free trips and reward points using the company's Visa signature card.

In May 1988, SW was the first airline to win the coveted Triple Crown for a month—Best On-time Record, Best Baggage Handling, and Fewest Customer Complaints. Since then, it has won more than thirty times, as well as five annual Triple Crowns for 1992, 1993, 1994, 1995, and 1996. The airline has contributed much to the advancement of the commercial airline industry.

Website: http://www.southwest.com/

Questions: What is the strategic advantage Southwest has used as the basis of its success? With Southwest's spectacular growth and profitability, what does the future hold for the company in light of the struggling industry as a whole?

CASE 15: WACHOVIA BANK

The banking industry has been going through a wave of mergers and acquisitions. The 2001 merger of First Union Corporation and the former Wachovia Corporation formed Wachovia. In 1753, Moravian settlers gave the name Wachovia to a tract of land they acquired in North Carolina. The settlers chose the name because the land resembled a valley along the Danube River known as Der Wachau. In 1879, a bank opened in the town of Winston under the name Wachovia National Bank.

According to its official material, "Wachovia Corporation is one of the largest providers of financial services to retail, brokerage and corporate customers, with retail operations from Connecticut to Florida and west to Texas, and retail brokerage operations nationwide. Wachovia had assets of $511.8 billion, market capitalization of $78.2 billion and stockholders' equity of $47.9 billion at June 30, 2005. Its four core businesses, the General Bank, Capital Management, Wealth Management, and the Corporate and Investment Bank, serve 13 million household and business relationships primarily through 3,126 offices in 15 states and Washington, D.C. A full-service retail brokerage firm, Wachovia Securities, and a Corporate and Investment Bank serves clients nationwide. Global services are offered through 40 international offices. Online banking and brokerage products and services are also available."

Like many American banks, Wachovia has pursued a growth strategy in the past few decades. Mergers and consolidation in the industry have occurred as banks moved to increase interstate and regional business. The thinking is clearly "bigger is better in tough competitive environments." The bank explained some of its strategic thinking in information to customers and shareholders. "Recently Wachovia acquired the international correspondent banking business of Union Bank of California (UnionBanCal), N.A. Through this transaction, it has integrated the Union Bank's sizeable international correspondent franchise, including 600 bank relationships, the payment and trade processing activity, which drives these relationships and the related loan book to an amount up to $2 billion. Union Bank has been strong in international correspondent banking for decades with a focus on the high-growth Asian market, where the bank established its first overseas representative office more than 40 years ago. As part of the transaction, a number of Union Bank's senior leaders, relationship managers and customer service and operations specialists have joined Wachovia's international team. Following completion of the transaction, the combined network has expanded Wachovia's coverage to include New Delhi, Chennai and Hanoi, cities where Wachovia is active but not currently represented. Wachovia will also gain Union Bank's more expansive menu of Yen-denominated transaction processing and credit services." While this is a success story, local banks may not have had the same experiences.

Website: http://www.wachovia.com/

Questions: Is Wachovia moving toward "global bank status" as its primary strategy? If not, should it be?

CASE 16: UNIVERSITIES AND COLLEGES

How do Oxford University, Pennsylvania State University and Dickinson College plan for the future? Some universities—Pennsylvania State University is one—have been engaged in strategic planning for several decades. The university uses a formal and elaborate system of planning procedures to define its critical issues, consider new directions and programs and address the many concerns of students, alumni, trustees, legislators and citizens of Pennsylvania. Here, the challenge is to create a participation model that is open but manageable. Integrating various curricula, while responding to local communities' needs, is a complex process in a system with 22+ campuses. Tension between centralization and autonomy is constant. The process at the university is open and public—unlike many private companies, which seek to keep their strategies and directions confidential. Many colleges and universities post their strategic plans on web sites to allow stakeholders to view promises and progress.

See: Strategic planning brochure and plan of Penn State University

Web site: Penn State University: www.psu.edu
        Oxford University: http://www.ox.ac.uk/
        Dickinson College: http://www.dickinson.edu/

Questions: How do we create a participative model for planning that incorporates views of faculty, students, alumni, and public? How much autonomy should be given to individual campuses to plot their own strategic directions?

CASE 17: NATIONAL ENERGY PLAN

Energy is vital, expensive and current supplies are stretched thin. In August of 2005, Hurricane Katrina tore through oil rigs and shut down key crude-oil refineries in the Gulf Coast region of the United States. In addition to natural events, some of the world's most unstable nations hold vast oil reserves: Saudi Arabia, Iran, Venezuela, Nigeria and Russia. Strife in any of them can send prices skyrocketing. In a tight market, even a refinery fire can raise prices. Disruption is potentially serious, because it means less oil to go around in an increasingly demanding world economy. Do we have an energy plan to address this threat?

The U.S., with just 5% of the globe's population, consumes 25% of its energy, and those figures are rising. We are setting new records for how much oil we import, now more than 10 million barrels a day. As developing countries' demand for oil increases simultaneously, the pressure on oil reserves will increase.

To reduce the consumption of oil, the government could increase taxes on oil products. Other solutions are the use of hybrid cars (that burn a mixture of fuel and electricity during combustion stage, leading to high mileage), renewable energy sources (solar, wind, biomass, geothermal and hydrogen fuel cell energy) or alternative fuels like ethanol, natural gas, propane, hydrogen, bio-diesel and methanol.

See Winik, L.W., "How High Can It Go?," *Parade* October 2, 2005

Website:
http://www.parade.com/articles/editions/2005/edition_10-02-2005/featured_0

Questions: What are the key threats to United States energy resources and what vision and strategies do we have for the future? How for example, can government promote the use of alternative or renewable fuel sources?

CASE 18: CENTRAL DAUPHIN SCHOOL DISTRICT

Public education is a critical resource in an increasingly technological society. The Central Dauphin School District (CD)—located in south central Pennsylvania—is the 13th largest school district in Pennsylvania and the largest of the 10 school districts located in the county. In its official material, CD states that there are nine school board members—citizens of the district—elected for four-year terms. In addition to these board members, "the 83,000 residents of the district serve on a variety of committees, e.g., curriculum, strategic planning, professional development, parent advisory, parent teacher association, and parent teacher/student organization."

The Central Dauphin School District spent two years developing the Strategic Plan. The CD Education Association appointed all administrators and teachers to the planning committee. Student council representatives were included. Subcommittees were created for addressing various segments of the plan, such as graduation requirements, culminating project, technology, assessment, etc. In addition, established committees, which already existed within the district, (e.g., Curriculum Review Teams, District Assessment Teams, Professional Development Education Committee and Special Services Teams) contributed to segments of the Strategic Plan that directly related to their areas of concentration. The Plan committee spent two years drafting the plan, including the mission statement, district beliefs and educational organizational goals. The involvement of many stakeholders contributed to the quality of the Strategic Plan.

Website: http://www.cdschools.org/cdsd/site/default.asp

Questions: What are the critical issues in public education and at what level should parents be involved in planning?

CASE 19: AMERICAN RED CROSS

Nonprofit organizations provide a broad range of services to citizens in need. Since its founding in 1881 by visionary leader Clara Barton, the American Red Cross has been the nation's premier emergency response organization. As part of a worldwide movement that offers neutral humanitarian care to victims of war, the American Red Cross distinguished itself by also aiding victims of devastating natural disasters. Over the years, the organization has expanded its services, always with the aim of preventing and relieving suffering.

The organization states that: "In addition to domestic disaster relief, the American Red Cross offers compassionate services in five other areas: community services that help the needy; support and comfort for military members and their families, the collection, processing and distribution of lifesaving blood and blood products, educational programs that promote health and safety, and international relief and development programs. Each year victims of some 70,000 disasters turn to the nearly one million volunteers and 35,000 employees of the Red Cross. Through nearly 900 locally supported chapters, more than 15 million people gain the skills they need to prepare for and respond to emergencies in their homes, communities and world."

Some four million people give blood through the Red Cross, making it the largest supplier of blood and blood products in the United States. The Red Cross helps thousands of U.S. service members separated from their families by military duty. As part of the International Red Cross and Red Crescent Movement, a global network of 181 national societies, the Red Cross helps restore hope to vulnerable people. An average of 91 cents of every dollar the Red Cross spends is invested in humanitarian services and programs. The Red Cross is not a government agency; it relies on donations of time, money, and blood to do its work. The Red Cross has processed financial assistance for hundreds of thousands of hurricane victims and provided relief support during the 2004 tsunami and other disasters.

Website: http://www.redcross.org/index.html

Questions. What are the critical strategic issues for the American Red Cross and what strategies will continue to move it forward?

Part 3

LESSONS OF PROGRESS, OUTCOMES & BENEFITS

Planning systems are often criticized for two weaknesses: (1) the way in which progress is assessed—if at all; and (2) the expected versus the realized outcomes and benefits of the planning system. Including this set of lessons in the learning package means we must think about the results of planning work at the *initiation* of strategy formation and *throughout* the process.

Planning for the long term requires a great expenditure of time and energy by senior executives with heavy short term operating responsibilities. When planning does not produce impact, these people have a legitimate complaint.

Learning this lesson provides an opportunity to win over the nay sayers who began the process with a cynical view. The lessons are organized around the following subjects:

- The plan,
- Psychological dynamics of the planning experience including risks, resistance to change, conflict, and frustration,
- Documenting real benefits and outcomes,
- The importance of action,
- A test of enthusiasm and appraisal by the participants.

These lessons present an opportunity to underscore the purposes and approach to strategy formation as a dynamic process. Planning activities must help the organization to identify and describe a vision of its future that all executives, managers, board members, and employees could feel excited about and become committed to.

PROGRESS ASSESSMENT

Lesson 60: Never once did we discuss how we are doing.

Baseball players have batting averages because they and their fans want to know how they are doing. Over time, data and standards define "good batting." The organization must use its plan and some guideposts to mark the way to the future. When planners do not assess how they are doing they miss opportunities to understand where adjustments must be made. Consider the Denver airport case reported by Ronald Henkoff.

> FINALLY, the much maligned automated baggage system at the much delayed Denver International Airport (DIA) was ready for its public debut. The switch was thrown. The TV cameras rolled. But what the viewers saw was a tornado of shredded suitcases and scattered clothing, evenCdon't look, childrenCan eviscerated Barney doll.
>
> More than one year behind schedule and more than $1 billion over its original budget, DIA, the first major airport built in the U.S. in 20 years, has become a world-class embarrassment. AIt's probably the most mismanaged place in America, complains Michael Boyd, president of Aviation Systems Research, a consulting firm in Golden, Colorado. AThey've built an airport that the airlines can't afford. Whenever the new field opensCthe latest target date is FebruaryCcarriers will have to pay operating costs of at least $18 per passenger, triple their costs at Denver's Stapleton Airport.
>
> Denver officials, beginning with former Mayor Federico Pena, now Secretary of Transportation, backed a baggage handling system so complex that it came to resemble a fighter plane designed by a congressional committee. Despite the problems, Mayor Wellington Webb remains optimistic: AThis will be the finest airport in the United States. It will also, he predicts, be the last one to be built for a very long time.

Many executives conduct a mostly ritualistic yearly review of their plan, only rarely do they engage in a "gut wrenching" evaluation of progress. An open discussion about progress is an uncomfortable experience, but an absolutely necessary one. The inability to reach goals because of external changes or internal failures on the organization's part is no crime by itself. The true failure—the real crime—is the failure to look at progress openly and directly—to ask simply, "How did we do this year?"

Progress assessment sessions can be held every six months or at least every year. When handled constructively, review is a motivating combination of "pats on the back" for progress achieved and clear identification of work that needs to be done; or work that needs to be done differently. Writing about strategic control issues, Michael Goold quoted two managers at ICI; one said: "We don't want to design a noose and ask people to put their heads in it." A Shell manager agrees: "Milestones must not be immutable. The dilemma is to get something between fixed goal posts and no goal posts." Executives, managers, board members and employees can emerge from a progress assessment session feeling very good that their future is closer than ever, but knowing that more work is ahead.

Illustration. Marston Community Mental Health Center engaged in a strategic planning process that required them to create a fairly different vision of the future in response to pressures from managed care companies. At six months and at year end the management team gathered for a short retreat to review progress; often a day and a half. The team concentrated on four aspects of progress; the number of clients served, revenue generated, new programs initiated, and the level of teamwork and interpersonal support among the management team.

The sessions were sometimes uncomfortable, often times supportive and on each occasion useful in determining how far they had gone to move into a future that was to be significantly different than their past.

Note(s)
Henkoff, R. "Smartest and Dumbest Managerial Moves of 1994." *Fortune.* Jan 16, 1995, p. 86.

DELAYED INSPIRATION

Lesson 61: Creative ideas may be a delayed result of the planning process.

Strategic planners began their work decades ago, hoping to see new ideas for products and services emerge full blown from the strategy making process. At the start of my strategic planning work nearly 30 years ago, I, too, thought the process was likely to generate significant new ideas for products, services, marketing, or even organizational structure. What I have found is a delayed effect. Few "brilliant ideas" popped effortlessly out of the standard strategic planning process. Instead, a good process "gets participants thinking." Weeks or months later the intersection of ideas proposed by various members of the group leads to creative directions and solutions to problems.

Illustration. Community Health System is a large multi-hospital health and medical services organization serving a community of almost 2 million citizens. As part of its strategic issues analysis, the group commented on growing competition and the need to become patient/customer friendly. Various ideas for new services were presented, as well as redesign of existing key revenue producers (e.g., cardiac care). No single proposal, large or small, seemed to stand out, but everyone was asked to think about patient centered services. Two months later nurses on the cardiac floor were complaining to the charge nurse and the attending physician about the difficulties of discharging patients by 11 a.m. (keeping patients past 11:00 meant billing for an extra day and tying up the bed). One nurse remarked that aside from the usual problems of obtaining timely last day lab results and physician review, the greatest problem was making sure the patient had transportation home. Another nurse said "why can't we take them?" There was no barrier other than the expense. Patient transport home for the cardiac care unit was started one month later. This patient friendly service proved enormously popular with patients and families, and the service helped with marketing and increased bed availability.

PLAN LENGTH

Lesson 62: The number of pages of the plan is inversely proportional to the number of readers.

This planning error has been mentioned indirectly a number of times. As the plan becomes more voluminous, fewer readers actually look at it. The planning process is not intended to create a huge document planners *hope* someone might read. Producing vision, decisions and actions is the goal; the paperwork documentation is merely a clerical exercise.

When a major document is produced, both planners and organization members begin to relate to the document itself, as opposed to the shared sense of the organization's future—the true outcome.

Several pages or a glossy brochure can present the major points of vision, mission, core products, services, and client groups. When done well, this document is used for both internal and external communications.

Illustration. In one of my first planning experiences, I helped to create a one hundred and fifty page plan for three counties that included everything from data to planning meeting summaries. Of the number of board members on the advisory group, I recall only one reading as far as page nineteen.

We have reviewed several universities' errors in producing a planning document whose length overwhelmed the potential readers. One university collected "local strategic plans" from its sixteen colleges (see Lesson 33). It received plans ranging from one hundred to one hundred and fifty pages and more. When college plans were combined the plan length was one of the most stunning barriers to readership ever constructed.

ORGANIZATION LEARNING UNCOVERED

Lesson 63: We learn collectively from successes and failures.

Organization learning—the acquisition, utilization and dissemination of data and knowledge—has been a growing topic of management and organization commentators. Strategic planning can be linked to organization learning through its efforts to understand what works and what does not (in the organization's present). The purpose of learning is to share data and knowledge about the company's products and services, production processes, marketing and so on. Recently, organizations are moving from "anything new must be invented" toward the discovery of product and service success in the "small corners of the enterprise." The idea is that somewhere within the company, product, market and service challenges have been met. We need only to create a culture and a process (of which strategic planning is one part) for discussion and sharing. One of strategic planning's core stages is understanding the company's present strengths and weaknesses.

Illustration. We can look for examples of organization learning in all industries, but one example of "failure to learn" seems particularly acute. The American auto industry is now facing stiff competition from foreign manufacturers. The result is decreasing sales, layoffs of longstanding employees and even distant threats of bankruptcy. While living off the significant profit margins from the sales of trucks and sport utility vehicles, American manufacturers failed to see the shift to smaller cars, higher gas prices and hybrid technologies. This is not a new problem, but one that was years in the making and which was foretold by earlier oil and gas shortages. Auto manufacturers failed to learn the lesson several decades ago and now must relearn.

In another example of learning deficiencies, the auto industry was confronted by defective tire/SUV rollover problems several years ago. Analysts found that both Ford and Firestone received early warnings of possible problems in foreign countries, but the learning was not transferred to auto and tire headquarters in the United States. The early opportunities for learning about the problem were missed.

PLAN PRIVACY—FEAR OR FEARLESS

Lesson 64: If we announce our plan, they will steal it.

Some leaders are afraid to announce their plans, fearing that they will be giving away proprietary strategy. Simultaneously, to be effective, the plan must be known and supported—widely. As an example, Jack Welch gave literally hundreds of presentations of vision and mission to employees at all levels of GE. Confident executives are fearless, relying on their organization's ability to execute faster and better than a competitor. Faster/better occurs when all stakeholders know where you are going and why.

Illustration. Hospitals are facing increasing competition. Ocean County Public Hospital proposed opening a new heart center, complete with specialty physicians, staff and a new facility. Fearing that nearby hospital competitors would jump at the chance to move faster, hospital executives kept details quiet. However, they failed to recognize that heart facility physicians had privileges at the competing hospitals as well. The physicians had discussed the plan and had realized that the competitors were not able to match the initiative. Unfortunately, many other hospital staff at Ocean were kept in the dark and were unable to contribute either energy or ideas to the new project.

EDUCATION

Lesson 65: "Just how does our organization work," we wondered. At the end of planning, we felt surprisingly educated.

How many executives, managers, board members, and employees assume that they fully know both the structure and the workings of their organization? Most would say they are informed about the core products and services, the authority structure, how it's managed, and "the way things are done"—the culture and climate. Surprisingly, open comprehensive planning can demolish these assumptions.

One truism noted by a great many management commentators is that the higher up you go in the organization, the more likely are subordinates to make two assumptions: (1) you are competent to handle things or your would not have risen to where you are; and (2) passing on bad news about what does not work is not good for one's career. The net result is that executives at senior levels are much less informed about the way their organizations truly work than they think they are because the flow of information up is rarely strong enough.

One benefit of a planning process conducted with open communication and dialogue is that managers, board members, and employees learn "how things really work." When the planning climate allows truly critical remarks about the downside of the organization—and all organizations have them—then learning increases. When criticism is presented in a constructive fashion and handled positively by the participants, everyone learns more about internal dynamics and structure. These learnings are critical because successful futures come from building on strengths and attacking weaknesses.

The lesson here is that no matter how educated you think you are, the planning process should truly deepen your understanding of the psychology, technology and structure of your private company or public agency. In this way, strategy formation contributes to the development of a learning organization.

Illustration. The Informatics Company had a history of strong planning. The executives chose to conduct a general strengths/ weaknesses analysis that would prelude a focused review of existing products and services. At this particular year in its multi-year planning process, planners focused on key areas of operating structure: hardware/ software products, education and training, customers and administrative support.

As the planners moved through the strengths/weaknesses analysis, it appeared that three programs were very strong and well thought of. However, three others seemed to be struggling—technical troubleshooting services, executive educational seminars, and legal support—not so much because of deficient staff performance, but due to unclear objectives.

Once the group became "educated" about the true needs of the organization, they focused their analysis. The group used its time to understand and propose changes to the three areas that seemed to need the most attention. Rather than celebrate wonderful past performance and how risk-free it would be to extend those strengths into the future, the planning group most productively used the time to attack weaknesses. They increased seminar planning and instructors, hired a consultant to assist information system hardware upgrading, and limited the legal advice to several key areas of litigation.

_____

RISK

Lesson 66: In the end—to play it safe—the group voted to do what it had always done.

One of the real indicators of the level of change proposed in the plan is the level of risk generated by the vision. If planners are truly interested in doing something different—in response to a radically changing environment—then there will be real risk associated with the change. The level of risk involved in the newly proposed programs, products or services becomes an indicator of how truly new the ideas are. When all the proposed actions feel pretty safe and no one is screaming, "But we might fail," the low risk indicates not very venturesome proposals.

As further evidence of status quo thinking examine the plan. Does it not look like the past simply extended? Planning participants will have opted for minimizing *risk* at the *cost* of pursuing truly innovative ideas.

Planners must avoid foolhardiness—pitching money, people, and resources at silly ideas is not a desired outcome of planning. But without new ventures the organization is trying to succeed with old approaches in a changed environment.

Illustration. At Old Hickory, a four year liberal arts college we discussed earlier, administrators and faculty focused their planning resources on the curriculum and support needs of undergraduate students, aged eighteen to twenty-two years. The organization considered itself to be serving this particular college market. At the close of year end planning, faculty and administrators felt they were making some useful adjustments to their vision of the future. The planners unconsciously but systematically denied that there were changes in the college environment—threats that increase the risk of doing nothing.

For example with the pool of eighteen-year-olds declining, it was necessary for Old Hickory to begin to think about serving an older population. Since the number of adults seeking continuing education programs was expanding dramatically, the adult student market presented a real opportunity. But by focusing on small incremental adjustments to the existing college curriculum the planners neglected to make changes to attract adults.

Other pressures were turned aside as well. At the national level there are discussions of education reform and changing views of curriculum content in the humanities and liberal arts areas. Some colleges are integrating humanities and liberal arts with professional studies. These changes too were ignored by the planners at Hickory.

A major overhaul of the college's educational system that included a radically revised curriculum and outreach programs for new student populations would be a better adjustment to the environment than the incremental change proposed. Since it would have created much more risk, it was avoided, even in discussion.

CHANGE RESISTANCE

Lesson 67: The resistance was based on ignorance of the CEO's plan (his plan, not *ours*).

The design of the planning system is intended to take into account resistance to change. Executives, managers, board members, and employees resist plans for the future when those plans have been created by someone else. Plans are blocked when there is little or no discussion with members of the organization. The principle is:

The level of resistance rises as the level of involvement falls.

If a CEO and one or two senior executives create a vision of the future, it is unlikely that that vision will advance for three reasons. First, board members, managers, and employees will at the very least not *understand* it. Second, they will decline to move aggressively to *support* it because it is not their plan. Third, they will actively *resist* the plan because they often do not agree with its content.

When plans are co-produced by executives, managers, board members and employees, resistance to "the plan" is reduced because the plan is a "joint plan." When large numbers of organizational participants have had an opportunity to co-produce the plan, it is not someone else's future that they are then asked to support but their own future. They have a stake in the outcome and have had an opportunity to help define and create it.

Unfortunately, too many organizations have learned the resistance lesson through failed plans. A brilliant plan created by a small group of hired planners, a select subset of broad members and executives, or by one dictator-style chief executive tends to meet with very high resistance indeed.

Another source of resistance is the existing structure of the organization, both policies and procedures and long-standing behaviors. Roger Martin writes:

> . . . few strategic plans are the victims of bad faith or employee slug-gishness. To use terms borrowed once again from Chris Argyris, it is rather that any newly *espoused* strategy, however explicit and sensible, inevitably comes up against an implicitly *enacted* strategy supported by all the aged, compounded steering mechanisms that the company already has in place.

Illustration. A physician executive leading Pennsylvania Health Maintenance Organization (PHMO) had a strong notion of what that company should be doing and where it should go in the future. He sent out memos that defined that vision—rapid national expansion—¥ for the employees and demanded that they implement it.

Some years later the physician executive was surprised to find that very little progress had been made. Screaming about the inactivism of corporate bureaucrats and the refusal to follow directions, the executive was figuratively stomping his feet and shouting:

"Why won't you do what I say?" "Where is my future?"

Company managers and employees were aware that the physician executive had presented his vision of the future. But it was not *their* vision and many felt that there were serious flaws in it. Without even a minimal opportunity to engage in dialogue about where the company was going, staff worked actively and passively to undercut the plan.

Note(s)
Martin R. "Changing the Mind of the Corporation." *Harvard Business Review* Nov/Dec 1993; p. 7.

BENEFITS

Lesson 68: We educated ourselves, but no vision, decisions or consensus emerged.

Most planning systems rest on the assumption that multiple benefits accrue to the organization as a result of the exercise. Board members and executives talk about the creation of vision, the set of decisions, the consensus on a shared future, and the education that participants receive as a result of planning.

However, some planning processes are *not* successful in leading the group to consensus, vision, or decisions. Sometimes these groups fall back on education as a defense, believing that the critical benefit is that executives, managers, board members, and employees have "learned" about their organization. While this may sound like "the learning organization" in operation, strategy formation as education alone is significantly short of results.

In summarizing his survey research of corporate planners, Professor Brian Houlden wrote:

> As far as the organization is concerned, the purpose of any corporate planner, or any corporate planning process, is to help it to choose its strategy. To choose strategy effectively involves diagnosing the major ('elephant') strategic issues and then analyzing them to choose which strategy to pursue. If a strategic planning process does not help with diagnosing these "elephants," or with analyzing them more than would be the case without the process, it is a cost without a benefit; it is not adding value and should be cut out. The same logic also applies to the corporate planners.

Just as we hold leaders responsible for bottom line impact, it is equally important to hold planning system designers responsible for ensuring that planners realize the intended benefits—a vision, consensus, strategy, decisions *and* education. Leaning on just process activities—good dialogue, strong participation, general information flow and open communication—is not enough to justify the extent of time and cost involved in a major planning process that uses significant executive, board member, and employee time.

Mapping the benefits to planning can be relatively easy. At the end of the year, planners put in writing the benefits flowing from the planning process during that year. If planners struggle with the task then there were probably fewer outcomes than hoped for.

Illustration. One academic department in a university medical school engaged in a planning process for the first time. After approximately three years, the department chose to conduct a review in conjunction with the Dean's planning updates. The department Chairman decided to provide to the core group of six planners and to the whole department faculty the actions and accomplishments that resulted from the first planning experience. What did he report?

The Chairman was able to identify a shared vision of departmental growth in research and clinical work (with consensus on some significant themes); a series of educational program actions and community service activities; improved clinical revenues and greater research grant income; and an expanded understanding of the department's management and financial performance procedures by the planning participants and by department faculty members. He was able to list in concrete terms what happened as a result of the planning process. Faculty participants also recognized the process, dialogue, and communication contributions but these were *in addition* to specific programmatic and managerial changes. (See also Lesson 63.)

Note(s)
Houlden, B.T. "How Corporate Planning Adapts and Survives." *Long Range Planning.* 28(4); 1995; 99-108.

MANAGEMENT EFFECTIVENESS

Lesson 69: At last, day-to-day decisions can be made to support the future.

This lesson is about the connection between strategy planning and what is increasingly labeled strategic management. What criteria do we use to make the day-to-day decisions regarding staff use, the expansion of programs or facilities, or the distribution of resources? One way to illustrate this connection between management and strategic planning is the famous quote used by many planners from Lewis Carroll's *Alice in Wonderland.* Alice is walking through the forest when she comes to a fork in the road. Wondering which way to turn she asks the Cheshire Cat.

> "Would you tell me please, which way I ought to go from here?"
> "That depends a good deal on where you want to get to," said the cat.
> "I don't much care where -," said Alice.
> "Then it doesn't matter which way you go," said the cat.

Alice, like many executives, has options. For executives and managers this fork in the road is defined in day-to-day terms as decisions on whether to spend money on staff, new product and service development, sales support, membership services or new facilities. How does the manager, like Alice, decide which road to take?

Management effectiveness is improved by planning when the vision of the future and the driving strategies are clear enough so that operating managers have criteria by which they can make decisions. When day-to-day decisions are driven by support of the organization's future then we increase management effectiveness in terms of building that future. This moves beyond planning to strategic management, i.e., making operations decisions in light of the strategic analysis and the new directions for the organization.

Illustration. After ten years, partnerships in a law firm known as Duncan, Smith & Jacobs became available as a result of retirements. These three openings represented an opportunity to address the firm's vision of the future—although it was not recognized at first by the thirty law partners.

One partner opened the discussion.

"Well, we are losing Martin, an experienced, successful litigator. We should obviously recruit another one."

A second said, "Since Sam (another retiring partner) was a corporate tax specialist surely we should recruit his replacement."

Still a third partner said, "If we are losing Mary our patent business leader we should recruit someone to take her cases and maintain the work load."

With ten percent of the partners turning over for the first time in a decade, the decisions were made almost in "no think" fashion. The new partners were to be aligned exactly as replacements. This was strategic management "ineffectiveness" if the error had stood uncontested. Because as a firm, Duncan Smith's future was to be different than its past—with less emphasis on corporate areas and a greater move toward two new fieldsCmedical malpractice and environmental law—the question of how to use the new partnerships was actually a strategic question. One partner stopped the group by raising the question.

"You know, I think the types of partners we select should depend on the type of firm we expect to have in the future, is that not true?"

With some discussion, the partners realized that in order to manage strategically they would have to match their newly selected lawyers with the desired future, particularly addressing expected new fields of business.

CHANGE ALL OVER

Lesson 70: Leaders planned a strategy only for new customers, and were surprised to find that the whole organization changed.

If strategic planning means planning for the *whole organization*, then we can expect that there will be changes not just in products and services but in management style, organization structure or even in the corporate culture. This lesson reinforces basic planning philosophy introduced in the first section. Planning aimed at just the technical side of the organization—the core services or products—is too narrow. For executives, expecting only to concentrate on the development of new lines of business or new customers the lesson is a surprising one. Christopher Reeves, chief executive of the Thomas Cook Group, comments on the sweeping changes generated by strategic competition.

> To meet all these imperatives—to become a world-class, 21st century company—the centre must be removed from most corporations. Then there will be no more battles between headquarters and the field, less hierarchy, more cross-border teams, and more senior managers who owe their position not to their rung on the ladder, but to portfolios of responsibilities that cross historical product, customer and geographic lines. This flattening of the organization must be forced, not in order to change the balance between headquarters and the field, but to create an organization that has no centre except its customers' needs, wherever the customers are.

The issue of whether *management* changes need to be made is often discomforting. In technically based firms—e.g. engineering companies, hospitals with large medical teams, computer systems companies—planners assume the targets are only their technical areas; engineering, medical care, computer systems. They are surprised to find that a new organization-wide vision of the future implies changes in organizing, leadership, control systems, reward structures, participation in decision making, and personnel. This raises the spectre of downsizing—the current fad. But as Marshall and Yorks note: "In planning any restructuring, managers need a link between the reorganization and the company's ongoing revitalization. . . . That link requires a strategic approach that enables executives to focus on making sure the organization has the right people in place after the reorganization is completed."

The lesson is that planning must provide for change "all over." Otherwise the planning is not really *organizational* planning but *market* and *technical* system planning with a much more limited contribution to the future.

There is however one note of caution. In discussions of strategy implementation, Hrebiniak and Joyce offer the "principle of minimum intervention." "In implementing strategy, managers should change only what is necessary and sufficient to produce an enduring solution to the strategic problem being addressed." We do not change purely for lack of better things to do.

Illustration. In large 570 bed Benton Community Hospital the senior management group was required by its accreditation society to create a redesigned and much more sophisticated quality improvement system. Hearing about the total quality management success of Deming, Juran and Crosby, the management team became very excited about the concept. They felt this was truly a way to make physicians and medical teams accountable for their use of resources and the quality of the care provided.

However, it was not until well into the development of the total quality management concept that the managers began to understand that *total* quality management was also about changing *manager* behavior, not just technical designs or professional communication among physicians and nurses. The managers were surprised to find that quality was becoming one of *their* major responsibilities. And they were unsettled by the need to make behavioral and structural changes in order to realize the vision of the organization's quality—improved future. Designing futures means not just changing one particular aspect of the organization (its practitioners of technology) but its managers as well.

Note(s)
Hrebiniak, L.G.; Joyce, W.F. *Implementing Strategy.* New York: Macmillan, 1984.
Marshall, R.; Yorks, L. "Planning for a Restructured, Revitalized Organization." *Sloan Mgmt.*
Rev. Summer 1994; 88-91.

ALL CONFLICTS SOLVED

Lesson 71: Never again did we argue about our future—also known as "the day the organization died."

Strategy formation is sometimes hoped to be a savior of organizational dynamics. In an organization racked with conflict, the planning process is viewed as a means to conflict resolution. With careful management and the use of some of the process to build teamwork, conflicts can be handled. There is another part of this lesson.

Conflict cannot and should not be totally removed from the organization. In organization behavior language, when conflict is removed "groupthink" prevails, a notion equally destructive to the strategic perspective of the organization. When captured by groupthink, executives, managers and board members are in general agreement about the way the firm works and why it is successful—from the vision to products and services. No one argues against ideas or projects, or proposes radical solutions that would offend the existing philosophical and operational positions because of the consensus. Decisions tend to be rubber stamped instead of being subjected to debate and discussion. A planning system that is working well should constructively surface and confront the conflict. And, it should do so in a way that establishes the substantive differences in the points presented by the different parties without enhancing the interpersonal confrontation of personalities.

Planning without conflict is an indicator of an organization dying. There must be enough new ideas, philosophies and directions to keep alive a vigorous debate. The direction of the organization's future and the day-to-day decisions that will help get the organization to that future must be open to inspection and analysis and they must include unexpected and unpopular proposals.

Illustration. In Polytechnic Institute's engineering department a number of the faculty had been trained by academic leaders from the same theoretical perspective. They gradually drifted into the group over a period of years because of the group support for this research and the mutual understanding of their positions.

However, during their education, students were exposed only to faculty ideas that seemed to flow in one direction, an established theme. Faculty meetings rarely contained much dissent because group members were oriented toward the same positions.

With the addition of five new faculty members, the concepts changed radically from engineering as applied problem solving to basic science research. Some of the new faculty members stimulated high levels of interpersonal conflict over research methodology and theoretical frameworks. The new approaches and subsequent conflicts were helpful in clarifying the department's direction for the future, although there were certainly aspects of the conflict that were hard to manage.

An effective planning system should build in an understanding of conflict and how it is effectively used to promote the organization's future.

ACTION

Lesson 72: Thoroughly discussed and beautifully written, the plan produced no action.

Planning must lead to action in the organization, otherwise there is no reason for the planning system to exist. Public agency leaders are often vulnerable to this weakness. Surely senior executives, managers, and board members have better things to do than print major documents to fill bookshelves. Operations employees detest visionary chatter with no impact. In private industry this is a common problem as well. Writing in the *Harvard Business Review* Roger Martin notes:

> I remember how in my earlier years as a consultant, the CEO and I would call urgent meetings, research customer needs from the bottom up, outline new and more efficient organizational structures and human resource policies, then articulate all of these findings as principles of action in a comprehensive voluminous strategic plan—only to find that these principles, if not open assaulted, died by a thousand cuts, while the strategic plan, if not openly rejected, was more or less systematically ignored.

This lesson targets the "bottom line" for planning.

Through my years of experience with planning systems, I have come to employ an action test of planning effectiveness. To examine the degree of impact we can ask: What areas of the organization change as a result of the planning process? Defining organizations as composed of five systems: (1) technologies (products, services, production and delivery system), (2) structure, (3)psychology, (4) management, and (5) corporate culture, I ask what actions will take place in each of these areas of the organization? A comprehensive, whole organization planning effort will result in some change in each system. I further explain that there are at least five action choices to result from the plan. In each system of the organization we look for what will be increased, decreased, maintained, started and/or what will be stopped. In relatively simple language and perhaps on one page, the group should be able to provide answers to the following sample questions.

- What new products and services will be started, which ones will be maintained, which ones will be stopped?
- How will the structure be altered?
- Will the psychology of the work place—e.g., quality of working life—be increased?
- How will the culture be maintained?
- What activities of management will be increased or decreased?

"Actions review" can be used in the auditing of the planning system. If the group struggles to convert their planning concepts to these action choices, probably the plan has too much abstraction and too little connection to operations. If, after a great struggle, the group still has much difficulty in defining what to do next, the planning process has not produced a clear path to the future.

Illustration. In working with a group of architects at the Grand Building Design Company some years back, I was convinced by the executive that he was truly interested in planning. Using a series of planning steps prior to a retreat, the planning group was able to establish some real priorities for action over the coming several years. The board of partners was very aggressive in offering solutions. However, in a discussion at the conclusion of the planning process, I asked the executive how he felt about the retreat. He suggested that it was okay, but did so in a discomforted manner. Probing a bit, I asked him what he actually felt about the process.

He said, "Well, the group went too far."

I asked him what he meant because the board proposed an exciting, ambitious plan which included restructuring of the organization, accumulation of financial resources, adding new products and services, and the design of a process for leadership transition.

His reply: "These are far too specific. I will need to spend the next year trying to 'undo' them!"

Although our discussion was never finished, it was clear that this executive was not really interested in seeing that planning leads to action. With his group *he* did the planning and constructed a vision. Following up board directed suggestions with actions to put their vision into place was not a desired outcome for the executive.

Note(s)
Martin, R. "Changing the Mind of the Corporation." *Harvard Business Review* Nov/Dec 1993, p. 7.

Operational Usefulness

Lesson 73: The plan was a work of art, suitable for framing, but not for following.

Some organizations produce plans much like beautiful annual reports. The glossy covers, the exquisite photography and the free flowing literature-like language, lull the reader into thinking that this is truly an impressive production.

However, the impressiveness of the production must be tied to the *operational usefulness* of the plan. The intended outcome of planning is not to produce art or literature. The plan must offer guidance for managers in day-to-day activities, linking strategic analysis with the behaviors to come. Strengths and weaknesses, vision and mission, strategies and program planning and resourcing activities that concern division and department managers are all one system. Without this linkage, the plan is useless.

Changes in strategy are reflected in the budget (see Lesson 56) which can be thought of as the operational plan for achieving the future. How operationally useful the plan is in connecting the strategic vision to day-to-day decisions is demonstrated by the degree of fit between decisions on capital and staff expenditures and movement toward the desired future.

Importantly, this means that the plan can often do without fancy graphics, coated paper, and literature-level writing.

Illustration. In the Soap Suds consumer product company, the chief executive and board members decided to use an outside planning consultation firm. The firm received a contract to develop scenarios of the organization's future including issues analysis, vision, strategy and resource requirements.

Key competitors were benchmarked to determine their market share, product costs and new product innovations. Pump style soap dispensers, environment-friendly chemical ingredients and heavy discounting through coupon distribution were uncovered and documented. Potential new product lines were identified and discussed in relation to the vision of the more diversified company. Meetings between senior executives and consultants were open and stimulating. A final report was concise, readable and exciting.

However, the organization neglected to create a process that would enable the organization's members to convert the long-term conceptual orientation into operational implications on a year-to-year basis. In short, there was no relationship between the long-term strategic scenarios and the operational decisions that truly concerned executives, managers, and employees on a daily basis.

The plan was completed at great expense and no action was taken.

TRIAL AND ERROR

Lesson 74: We expected planning perfection on the first try and were disappointed.

Many organizations expect that they will be able to run the planning system efficiently and effectively the first time through. But for many executives, managers, board members, and employees, a formal planning system that actually works is a trial and error experience that becomes stronger over a period of years. There is a learning curve to be traveled as participants increase their understanding and "practice" the strategy formation process. This lesson is about expectations.

Several parts of the process always seem to be at the center of learning experiences. Mission review frequently is an interminable process without a satisfying conclusion. Openly confronting weaknesses and progress failures tests the degree of trust and openness in the culture. Participants confuse vision and grand strategy with short-term operational planning. Each organization needs to become comfortable with the purpose and outcomes of each part of the process. Mission comes to have meaning; weaknesses are confronted without firings and the strategic plan is followed by an operational plan.

Reporting on his research on strategic planning systems, Professor Brian Houlden presented these comments. "Responses to my questionnaire which convey the changes in the corporate planning process included "from budget-driven to mission, objectives, strategies and tactics and environment"; "more creative and less financial"; "greater line responsibility for planning"; "becoming more pro-active"; "less focus on number checking and financial analysis"; "more focus on key issues"; "responsibility for plans more decentralized"."

Although many planning consultants, academics and other experts would have us believe that super-class planning systems can be created and implemented without flaws and adaptation, this is not true. When executives and board members purchase assistance in planning system design, most understand that there will be adaptations and improvements needed.

Illustration. Many organizations use planning retreats with several purposes in mind. As one phase of trial and error learning, the planning retreat can be used to teach the members of the organization about the planning process.

For example, in the past few years, I've worked with bankers, engineers, physicians, contractors, public health workers, psychologists, nurses, and public administrators in retreats. In almost all cases, the participants thought they understood what the process was about. However, by the end of the retreat (and through trial and error) they had a much better sense of what worked in their particular culture and what did not.

Note(s)
Houlden, B.T. "How Corporate Planning Adapts and Survives." *Long Range Planning.* 28(4); 1995; 99-108.

CONTINUITY

Lesson 75: Each year we produce an original scenario of the future with a hot new technique known as Strategic ZigZag.

Planning in complex organizations leads to visions that require time and effort to put into place. A lesson that some organizations seem not to be learning is that we do not produce a new strategic vision with strategy to match each year.

The whole concept of long-term thinking—less attention to quarterly results and short-term payoffs—means that organizations must build continuity into their organizational visions and daily operational decision making. This is not an easy thing to do, particularly with changes in leadership at various levels of the organization. Continuity of vision and strategy is necessary because executives, managers, board members, and employees understand the difficulty of moving an organization in even a slightly different direction. The concept of creating a future and attaining it in six months is an obviously silly one. But this silly idea is unconsciously embraced by far more leaders than we would care to believe.

Perhaps the best way to talk about continuity is to hear one example. In writing about strategic vision Ian Wilson used the CEO of General Electric as an example.

> From the day that Dr. John F. Welch, Jr., took over as General Electric's (GE's) CEO from Reginald H. Jones, he articulated, strongly, clearly and constantly, a vision for the company that stressed two elements: a restructured portfolio and a revitalized culture. He has consistently implemented these two elements in tandem, although, for the first 6 or 7 years, portfolio restructuring was the first priority. Only in the past 2 or 3 years has revitalizing the culture become the dominant theme.

The tough question is how does one maintain a vision in the face of both internal organizational changes and environmental turbulence. Continuity means support through successive environmental threats and internal changes.

Continuity in the public sector seems to be even more challenging. Potential turnover of political leaders means public agencies may face a fourth year sunset of their vision. Somewhere in between private and public are the utilities companies. Patricia Eckert, Commissioner with the California Public Utilities Commission discussed the need for a longer term vision to push change while facing a continuous stream of short-term proposals (that amount to incremental adjustments to the status quo).

Our collective impatience means that futures that emerge through continuous support over five to ten to twenty year periods are those that have the leaders' continuity of vision to ensure that they actually happen.

Illustration. Sometimes an organization loses continuity because of the barriers it faces in implementing its vision. For example, the state funded colleges mentioned in other illustrations faced a political period when capital improvements were eliminated. For many of these state universities, the budgeting problem was a temporary setback in their path to become larger, more capable universities. To see this setback as a reason to change their vision of their future would be to abandon the continuity that is needed to ensure that the future comes about.

In Harrisburg, Pennsylvania, the mayor is demonstrating continuity and perseverance in its plan to develop a dam along the Susquehanna River. The Mayor believes raising the water level of the one mile wide river three to five feet would open all sorts of additional recreational and economic development opportunities. Environmentalists fear that the dam would disrupt wildlife habitats and so have fought plans for *ten* years. But the Mayor continues his fight to gain the necessary clearances because he believes in the vision of a city with recreational water space as strategic advantage. This will not happen quickly.

POST ACTION REVIEWS

Lesson 76: In order to learn, we must reflect on process and outcome.

Here, we borrow from the military a technique long used in battle operations circles (see Darling, Parry, Moore "Learning in the Thick of It"). To generate organization learning in tight time requirements, the military uses "after action reviews." Participants are asked to consider the characteristics of recent actions that led to success or failure. No large reports are made. Analyses of the "learnings" are rapidly disseminated to colleagues.

Illustration. Wadley and Simpson is a full service clinical psychology and psychiatry practice located at the edge of a major eastern city. Founded by two friends—a clinical psychologist and a psychiatrist, the practice is now twenty years old and booming. Realizing the need for expansion space and with an interest in capturing continuing growth, the partners decided to open a satellite office in a suburban area about 15 miles away. The area was growing rapidly with many young professionals and new families. Other than renting an office suite, relatively little was required for the expansion, since the staff used mostly independent contractors. Founding partners agreed to be on site 1-2 days per month. After a two year trial, they met with senior clinicians to discuss the low level of client demand. On the agenda for discussion was marketing, fees, and most important, client needs. After review, they found there was not a sufficient level of business to continue the new effort. The satellite unit was closed.

Note(s)
Darling, Parry, Moore. "Learning in the Thick of It." *Harv. Bus Rev.* July-August, 2005

DEMONSTRATING BENEFITS

Lesson 77: When a new board member asked for the top three benefits of planning, we stared at the ceiling and squirmed in our chairs.

A new member of the planning group—executive, board member, manager, employee—can sometimes ask a very simple question:

> What exactly do we get for the time and energy we are devoting to the planning process?

Unfortunately, some organizations find themselves confronted with the impact statement presented in Table 1 (see next page).

Throughout this book we have discussed the benefits, including a vision of the future, decisions regarding how to get into that future, education for the participants, and an increase in teamwork. The challenge of stating in concise language the benefits resulting from the planning process is an important exercise.

The benefits can go beyond numbers of new clients, revenue increases or growth in market share, as noted in the *Economist*.

> Managers spend too much time looking at published results and not enough looking at what drives those results. Most chairmen know their company's overall return-on-sales. Surprisingly few know what percentage of their products are delivered on time or what the age-profile of their machinery is. Such figures are often not even collected. That is rather as if a tennis player watched the scoreboard, but not the ball.

If the planners struggle to demonstrate the benefits of planning and can list few changes, the planning system needs work.

Illustration. A small entrepreneurial Rug Company has an informal planning system. The chief executive and his partners use their annual planning retreat as a way to review their progress from the previous years. Part of their strategic discussion is, how did the planning system serve us over this period of time?

In an earlier illustration I noted that one academic department chairman took the opportunity of a three year review to identify the benefits of the planning process to that point. This is a good exercise even when it is a struggle.

Table 1.

THE BENEFITS OF PLANNING

Could your planners and strategists identify the contribution of planning to the organizational growth and development at the end of the year? If that cannot be done very easily with a combination of both qualitative and quantitative impacts, then the benefits of planning are weak. The planning system is in need of redesign.

PERIODIC PROGRESS REVIEW PROCESS

Lesson 78: Require regular progress reports in a low tech, highly visible process.

One of the faults of traditional planning processes is how and when to report on progress toward the desired future. Report too soon and you risk showing no impact because it is too early in the process.

Major strategy shifts take a while to engage. Report too late in the process and participants feel like the leaders do not care about progress. The solution is to devise an easy-to-use periodic process for reporting progress. One low tech solution is to have leaders of various parts of the strategy provide brief presentations on their unit's progress toward the future. By brief, I mean one slide and 15 minutes, maximum.

Illustration: A clinical department in a Western Medical School initiated what turned into a ten year series of strategic planning sessions and an annual retreat. With about 50 faculty physicians, the Department was small enough to hold a "whole group meeting." At the start of the second year, the chairman considered how to report progress to his faculty. With four division chiefs—education, clinical, research and administration—He decided to have his four division chiefs—education, clinical, research and administration —report at the annual retreat, but limited them to one slide and fifteen minutes each. Each division chief prepared thoroughly as the presentation was made to 50 faculty colleagues and occasional outside guests, such as the Dean. This low tech reporting process proved extremely effective in communicating progress and in stimulating continuous movement.

FULL SPECTRUM REPORT CARDS

Lesson 79: Since strategic planning includes the "whole organization", report cards should too.

Strategic planning began life as a financial exercise. The concept was to identify the current strengths and weaknesses of the organization's product line and services from a financial perspective. As such, it was the purview of the chief financial officer and his/her staff. Significant time was spent scanning the outside environment for threats and opportunities—financial for the most part. Staff busied themselves running quantitative analyses of the financial health of the organization—both private companies and large private non-profit organizations. As the sense of "designing the future" expanded, strategic planning became more of a general management exercise involving production managers and technical staff, human resources, marketing and sales.

Illustration. American Health Inc. is a very large health insurance company which continues to see strategic planning as a financial exercise. A small strategic planning staff reports to the chief financial officer (CFO), paying almost exclusive attention to market share, revenues, profit margins and capital expenses for new initiatives. When asked about the future organization—its culture, climate, and attitudes toward customers and employees—the CFO said "that's not my responsibility."

CALL FOR MORE

Lesson 80: When we asked for several dates for the next planning session, the room was silent.

A test of the success of the planning system is how eager are the planning participants to engage in the next round? Although I have not had the experience of having *no one* willing to talk about the next planning session's date, I have had the opposite experience-eagerness. Creating interest in more requires that you "pop the champagne cork" to celebrate previous success. If as William Sandy puts it "Nothing happens when you win" your team is unlikely to get excited about the next competitor.

If planning participants are enthusiastic about the next series of sessions, they have a "gut level" feeling that the planning process is both interesting and worthwhile. When planning participants express willingness to participate in more planning it means the time and energy expended was worthwhile.

In considering the role of top management in strategy formation, Bartlett and Ghoshal cite the philosophy of Anita Roddick, founder of the U.K.-based beauty products retailer The Body Shop. Roddick says,

> Most businesses focus all the time on profits, profits, profits. I think that is deeply boring. I want to create an electricity and passion that bonds people to the company. Especially with young people, you have to find ways to grab their imagination. You want them to feel they are doing something important. I'd never get that kind of motivation if we were just selling shampoo and body lotion.

The strategy formation process and the vision should catch the imagination and fire up the staff for action.

Illustration. While working with a group of highly successful professionals for the first time, we experienced as much resistance to the planning concept as to the new ideas proposed. This particular group—International Engineers Ltd.—had never engaged in formal planning before and thought it was basically a bureaucratic waste of time. However, after a series of planning sessions and a multi-year period of action, we conducted a review session. At the end of the review of the planning benefits the planning participants suggested spontaneously: "This was really great, we should do more of this," an exact reversal of the college administrator's experience in the earlier illustration. When planning participants begin with resistance, and end with a call for more, then the planning system has made the grade.

A strategy formation process that "makes the grade" is dependent on three components: structure of the strategy process, the successful functioning and dynamics of strategy creation work and the outcome. While structure and process can make us feel good and ask for more, it is the outcome of the strategy that we ultimately seek. H. Wayne Huizenga, a billionaire dealmaker has demonstrated "strategy outcome" at the highest level. He built two companies—Waste Management (garbage collection) and Blockbuster (video rentals)—into two stunning examples of commercial success. He is now building a third company, a conglomerate called Republic Industries. We have limited public information about the structure and process of his strategy formation work but we can see the outcome. When he calls a strategy meeting people come.

Note(s)

Bartlett, C.A.; Ghoshal, S. "Changing the Role of Top Management: Beyond Strategy to Purpose." *Harv. Bus. Rev.* Nov-Dec 1994; 84-85.

Sandy, W. "Avoid the Breakdowns Between Planning and Implementation." *J. Business Strategy.* Sept-Oct 1991.

CASES

___

CASE 20: HARRISBURG INTERNATIONAL AIRPORT

Efficient airline transportation depends upon updated airports with sufficient capacity to serve growing numbers of passengers. Harrisburg International Airport (HIAA) was created under the ownership of the Commonwealth of Pennsylvania and has been serving Central Pennsylvania for over 100 years. The Commonwealth transferred ownership to the Susquehanna Area Regional Airport Authority in 1998. The Authority board uses volunteers appointed to staggered, five-year terms from Cumberland, Dauphin, and York counties, the cities of Harrisburg and York, and Fairview and Lower Swatara townships.

In their description the HIAA notes these key facts. Approximately 1,400 people work within the airport system of Harrisburg International, Capital City, and Franklin County Regional Airports. The employees are working to create hometown airports with national and international connections. HIA provides transportation facilities for public limousines, taxi, car rental, and CAT. Amenities include free wireless Internet, diverse food concession choices, from fast food to snacks to sit-down restaurants, in both pre- and post-security locations. Frequent fliers—those logging 25,000+ miles per year on any airline servicing HIA—can take advantage of the Susquehanna Club, an airport-run frequent flier lounge. The airport provides assistance for travelers with disabilities, including accessible parking, special handicap accessible buses, elevators and wheelchairs.

Website: http://www.flyhia.com/

Questions: What are the obstacles to plans for expansion of small airports such as HIA, given regulatory and public resistance, security issues and strong competition from larger city airports?

CASE 21: WEST SHORE LIBRARY

Libraries are a focal point for communities, serving a diversity of customers from young students to seniors. In 1960, the Cumberland County Commissioners used Pennsylvania State County Library to begin a county library system. From a modest start, further federal grants helped the county to meet state standards, hire staff, maintain a union catalog and manage outreach programs for underserved residents. Responding to significant growth, the library was renovated in 2001. The building provides 5500 square feet of space and houses administrative, information technology, technical, outreach, and training services. The library offers centralized technical services (acquisitions, cataloging, and processing). Members of the library can access a wide range of information and data providers, including: Gale Net, Heritage Quest, World Atlas, World Book Online, and Prescription for Information (Consumer Health Information). Homebound delivery service is provided to Cumberland County adult residents who are unable to visit the library regularly due to age, illness or disability. It also offers kits of programming materials to people who plan and provide programs for older adults. The materials are available for use by nursing homes, senior centers, retirement complexes or any Cumberland County Library System cardholder.

Website: West Shore Camp Hill library: www.ccpa.net/ls

Questions: As all libraries, this one has had to confront the challenges of rapidly changing technology and increasing sophistication of its users—all within constrained budgets. What should be the vision and strategy for the library's future?

CASE 22: PHILADELPHIA PUBLIC HOUSING

Housing is a core need for all citizens. The Philadelphia Housing Authority (PHA) was established in 1937 and is the nation's fourth largest housing authority. It is the biggest landlord in Pennsylvania, primarily funded by the federal government. In the Authority's material, the mission and activities are clear: "They develop, acquire, lease and operate affordable housing for city residents with limited incomes. Working in partnership with the city and state governments, as well as private investors, PHA provides around 800,000 people with homes." Two thousand people are employed to deliver services to their clients with a total budget of $350 million. PHA has established over 40 developments, including 6,400 scattered housing units. Supervised by a five-member Board of Commissioners (two appointed by the Mayor, two appointed by the City Controller, and one appointed by the other four members of the Board), the Philadelphia Housing Authority recently accepted a $17 million grant from the U.S. Department of Housing and Urban Development (HUD) for the planned redevelopment of the Ludlow neighborhood in North Philadelphia. The HOPE VI award will be used to build 100 new homes.

Website: http://www.pha.phila.gov/home/default.aspx

Questions: As a public-private venture, the housing authority aims to provide low cost, quality housing for citizens in need. How successful is public housing in providing the best housing (in terms of quality of living and cost) for needy people? What are the unique strategic issues in this partnership?

CASE 23: AMERICAN HOSPITAL ASSOCIATION

The hospital industry has long operated as a mixed economy—part private sector, part public sector. Hospitals need to work collaboratively to influence their business environment. In September 1899, eight hospital superintendents met in Cleveland to discuss common concerns and interests, which led to the formation of the Association of Hospital Superintendents. In 1906, with some changes in membership rules, its name was officially changed to the American Hospital Association.

The founding of Blue Cross in 1937 was a major achievement of AHA. Blue Cross helped standardize care services and solve the funding for the Commission on Hospital Care, the recommendations of which led to establishment of the Hill-Burton program. The AHA was instrumental in establishing national recognition of the special health care problems of the elderly, contributing to the breakthrough

Medicare legislation of 1965. AHA was an early advocate of prospective pricing for Medicare reimbursement and set the pace for understanding and eventual congressional passage of a prospective pricing system.

AHA is the national organization that represents and serves all types of hospitals, health care networks, and their patients and communities. Around 4,800 institutional and 33,000 personal members form the AHA. AHA focuses on projects that demonstrate innovations in health care service structure and delivery. They offer educational programs, and conduct data collection and analysis to identify trends and develop policy. Publications keep members informed of national developments and trends and their impact on local communities. Professional development for health care managers are two other key functions.

Website: http://www.aha.org/

Questions: Is the strategic goal of the AHA to enhance the efficiency and effectiveness of the American healthcare industry, or is its primary duty to advance the professional and commercial interests of its institutional and personal members? How would a strategic plan advance both interests?

CASE 24: UNIVERSITY OF PENNSYLVANIA BOOKSTORE

Book publishing and sales have always been competitive. Universities seek both profits and services from the stores on campus. On April 22, 1996, University of Pennsylvania President Judith Rodin announced the development of a 50,000 square foot superstore in partnership with Barnes & Noble. Barnes & Noble, the nation's oldest and largest retail bookseller, currently operates more than 300 campus bookstores and approximately 370 superstores across the country. The Barnes & Noble superstores are modeled after the company's "Main Store" in New York City, the world's largest bookstore.

The store's material described the new structure: "In September 1998, after the construction, it carried around 130,000 book titles; up to 2,000 periodicals, magazines, foreign publications and newspapers; an academic technology and multimedia center; a comprehensive music department with listening boards; a cafe; and comfortable seating areas." Under the terms of the partnership, Barnes & Noble College Bookstores paid approximately half of the estimated $8 million construction costs. It later expanded to an assortment of emblematic clothing and gifts, dorm supplies, class rings, a large poster and print department, and art and engineering supplies. It had enhanced discounting policy, including 20 percent off all hard covers, 30 percent off New York Times hardcover bestsellers, and up to 90 percent off on bargain books.

The addition of the Barnes & Noble superstore to the University of Pennsylvania community contributed to changes in campus life. The partnership benefited the bookseller, students, and the citizens of Philadelphia. The agreement with Barnes & Noble College Bookstores is also an innovative way for the university to generate additional revenue, exemplifying a strategic investment that will yield long-term benefits.

Websites: University of Pennsylvania : www.upenn.edu
             Barnes and Nobles: www.barnesandnoble.com

Questions: Does this type of bookstore unfairly compete with the business of individual bookstores? Except books, most of the items for sale in the bookstore are overpriced. Is it justifiable from both the student and university perspectives? Should universities use the bookstore model as a way to expand their strategic partnerships with the private sector? What are the pros and cons of this strategy?

CASE 24: GOOGLE

Internet services and products have revolutionized society in the last 10-15 years. What are the future challenges for this new industry? Larry Page and Sergey Brin started building the Google search engine while they were graduate students at Stanford University in 1996. After developing an effective search engine, they were financed by Andy Bechtolsheim, one of the founders of Sun Microsystems, who was used to taking the long view.

What are they doing now to extend their success? Recently Google Print announced agreements with the libraries of Harvard, Stanford, the University of Michigan, the University of Oxford, and the New York Public Library to digitally scan books from their collections to enable users worldwide to search them in Google. In 2005, Google offered Google Mini, a smaller and lower-cost solution for small and medium-sized businesses that want Google quality searches for their documents and sites. Google Video was also launched—a new project that captures the closed-caption information on TV programming and makes it searchable.

Google's Image Search has grown to contain more than one billion images of all types—photos, drawings, paintings, sketches, cartoons, posters, and more. The latest version of Google Desktop Search now has the ability to locate many more file types, including PDF and MP3. It's available in English, French, German, Spanish, Italian, Dutch as well as Chinese, Japanese and Korean. Another new feature launched in Google Local is Google Maps, a dynamic online mapping feature that can find location information and get directions quickly and easily.

Website: www.google.com

Questions: Will concerns about privacy be the most important external challenge for this company? How important are fears of censorship in its new markets e.g. China? How does an organization insure it has the imagination and capability to survive and thrive in technologically dynamic and hotly competitive industry?

CASE 26: NATIONAL GEOGRAPHIC

The National Geographic magazine is about 118 years old. It continues to have a strong position among specialty publications and expects to flourish going forward. In 1998, an editorial raised some interesting strategic questions for the magazine's leaders and staff writers. "Why don't you call your magazine International Geographic?" is a question that Editor Bill Allen often receives. His reply: "We get letters asking that question all the time, and while it's probably best that we stick with the name that has served us so well for 110 years, there's no question that the global scope of our readership is light-years beyond that of our first issue, when only 31 of our 217 Society members lived outside the District of Columbia"

[United States]. Today the magazine is published in Japanese, with editions also serving Spain, Latin America, Italy, Greece and Israel.

Website: National Geographic: http://www.nationalgeographic.com/
National Geographic Magazine:
    http://www7.nationalgeographic.com/ngm/0602/index.html

Questions: How strategically important is the name of the magazine to the publication's mission? What strategic gains are found in branching out to other languages? How strongly focused should the marketing efforts be and does the international distribution affect content?

CASE 27: COUNCIL OF SCIENCE EDITORS

Many of us belong to an organization or professional society that represents our collective commercial and craft interests. Just like physicians, lawyers, electricians and architects, editors also have such an organization. Editors with an interest in the biology and medicine fields began a Society in 1957 by joint action of the National Science Foundation and the American Institute of Biological Sciences. Today, the group enjoys close relationships with a number of scientific publishing organizations, both national and international, but they function autonomously, relying on the vigor of more than 1,200 members to achieve the goals of the organization.

Known for some years as the Council of Biology Editors, leaders of the group began to discuss their intention to grow beyond the limits of their single discipline. In the 1990's, a task force was formed to consider the history, mission and mandates of the organization and thus the Council of Biology Editors (CBE) became the Council of Science Editors on January 1, 2000. Out of a strategic planning process came the decision to expand membership boundaries—indicated by a name change to the Council of Science Editors. With the change, social science editors and others could join the membership. This represented a "strategic leap" for the society, one that had both short-term and long-term impact.

Web sites: http://www.councilscienceeditors.org/about/history.cfm
        http://www.councilscienceeditors.org/index.cfm

Questions: How is strategic planning different for a professional society where the members have their own individual interests? Is there a common approach to planning in professional societies and associations?

CASE 28: SMITHSONION INSTITUTION

The Smithsonian Institution (SI) is a premier museum system and supporter of scientific research and exploration. Located in Washington, D.C., the organization, with its collection of national museums, is at once the "nation's attic" and the guide to the future based on learning from the past. Founded in 1826, the museum draws millions of visitors each year for exhibits on air and space, natural history and memorabilia of all sorts relating to America's founding and history. Although the Smithsonian Institute enjoys a strong tradition and solid record of financial and human resource support, it, too, faces questions about the future. Unlike smaller museums (such as the Pennsylvania State Museum), the Smithsonian is expected to be a national leader, offering cutting edge ideas on how to provide high quality museum experience and support scientific exploration and research.

Web site: http://www.si.edu/

Questions: What are some of the important issues facing the SI from outside the institution? How does politics play a part in determining its future? What areas of the SI would you examine to assess its current strengths and weaknesses? What constitutes an exciting vision of the SI future?

CASE 29: LONG TERM CARE—WALNUT HILL

Long term acute care is facing strong pressures on both the cost and quality fronts. And over the next several decades, long-term care will likely also face strong market demand for increased services. Consider the introduction to one long-term care plan.

"The Walnut Hill Continuing Care Retirement Community developed a strategic plan to help guide it through a restructuring and improvement process that enhances service by improving response to internal and external changes. The planning group considered the organization's mission and philosophy, analyzed future directions, examined internal and external issues, and developed a series of strategies and actions that will make them responsive to those issues for the next five years.

The facility's primary mission is to develop a responsive and effective clinical and social support program that addresses the emotional, social, psychological, and physical needs of all clients.

The organization's desired future is different from its current situation in six ways: (1) insufficient quality assurance; (2) inadequate service delivery integration; (3) low staff morale; (4) a decreasing number of potential nurse aides; (5) relatively few relationships with the greater community; and (6) inadequate computer technology and staff capacity.

The planning team recognized external issues, including: (1) the aging of the Walnut Hill population; (2) the trend for lower-paid workers to move to other areas, seeking better jobs; (3) potential competition in the assisted living area; and (4) the formation of a grassroots aging advocacy group.

The critical needs for WHRC included internal development and external linkages. These areas will be addressed first. Strategies to be adopted by WHRC include: (1) addressing quality concerns through continuous quality improvement teams, beginning with concerns in the nursing home facility; (2) determining the various service, programs, and administrative tasks in all of the CCRC units, in order to identify areas where greater integration would benefit clients, staff and the organization as a whole; (3) developing and implementing a survey regarding staff morale and ways to address staff concerns; (4) addressing relationships with outside organizations, including the statewide organization that assists skilled nursing facilities to contract with managed care organizations, the aging advocacy group, and the potential developers of a competing assisted living facility; and (5) identifying computer-related needs and building additional technology funding into the budget."

See: Mara, C.M.; Ziegenfuss, J.T. "Creating the Strategic Future of Long-Term-Care Organizations." *Care Management Journals*. Vol. 2 Number 2; Summer 2000, pp.116-124.

Web site: Select a web site of a local long-term care facility

Questions: What is different about an organization designed to serve older patients? How will the larger demographic changes (i.e. aging of the population in many countries) affect the set of opportunities and threats to long term care organizations?

CASE 30: THE UNITED NATIONS

The United Nations (UN) officially came into existence on 24 October 1945, when China, France, the Soviet Union, the United Kingdom, the United States and a majority of other signatories ratified the founding charter. In their official statement, they describe their mission and activities: "The United Nations is an international organization of 191 sovereign states, representing virtually every country in the world. Member states are structured by the principles of the UN Charter, an international treaty that spells out their rights and duties as members of the world community. The central role of the United Nations is the promotion of peace and security, development and human rights around the world."

Presently the UN's goal is to help to envision and realize the "Millennium Declaration." Passed in September 2000 by more than 150 presidents, prime ministers and other world leaders , this declaration targets areas of peace, security and disarmament; development; environmental protection; human rights, democracy and good government; protecting the vulnerable; meeting the special needs of Africa; and strengthening the UN.

Website: http://www.un.org/english/

Questions: There have been significant questions about the ethics, structure and viability of the UN. Will restructuring be the lead strategy for enacting a new vision of the UN future? How can we redesign the organization to address the corruption and other scandals plaguing the organization?

CASE 31: WORLD BANK

In international development circles, one financial institution stands out. Here is their history and structure as they define it. "The World Bank (WB) was established on July 1, 1944 during a conference of 44 countries in Bretton Woods, New Hampshire. Approximately 184 countries are members with the headquarters located at Washington, DC, and more than 100 country offices (approximately 10,000 employees in offices around the world). The World Bank includes the International Bank for Reconstruction and Development (IBRD) and the International Development Association (IDA). Each institution plays a different but supportive role in the effort to reduce global poverty and improve living standards. The IBRD focuses on middle income and creditworthy poor countries, while IDA focuses on the poorest countries in the world. The World Bank does not operate for profit. Major affiliates of the World Bank are the International Finance Corporation (IFC), Multilateral Investment Guarantee Agency, and International Centre for Settlement of Investment Disputes (ICSID)."

The WB offers grants to facilitate development projects, relieve the debt burden of heavily indebted poor countries, improve sanitation and water supplies, support vaccination and immunization programs, combat the HIV/AIDS pandemic etc. The WB also offers analytic and advisory services to its member countries. Another core Bank function is to increase the capabilities of its own staff, its partners and people in developing countries. WB Global Development Learning Network is an extensive network of distance learning centers that uses advanced information and communications technologies to connect people working in development around the world.

In 2004, the World Bank provided $20.1 billion for 245 projects in developing countries worldwide. The bank is currently involved in more than 1,800 projects in virtually every sector and developing country. The projects are as diverse as providing micro credit in Bosnia and Herzegovina, raising AIDS-prevention awareness in Guinea, supporting education of girls in Bangladesh, improving health care delivery in Mexico, helping East Timor rebuild following independence and India rebuild Gujarat after a devastating earthquake.

Website: http://www.worldbank.org/

Questions: What are the key strategic issues facing the World Bank in a shifting and uncertain worldwide political environment? Could the WB do more to foster development in emerging countries as a part of their extended vision? And, if so, what key strategies and programs should they offer?

CASE 32: COUNTRY PLANS

We know that at the country level, centralized planning is a "dead approach" to building economic and social viability. But how do we begin to sketch a vision of the future at the country level? And, could we use this approach to assist developing regions and multi-country linkages (e.g., European Union) as well as newly emerging nations such as Iraq? In western democracies, this vision building process more or less emerges as part of political campaigns.

In some elections, several key issues seem to drive the debate as opposed to a more general discussion of where the leaders would like to take the country and how they would like to guide them. There has been some discussion of the need to create a countrywide dialogue about the future, including issues of values, technology, education, crime and defense for example.

See: Ziegenfuss, J.T. "Can America have a beautiful future? Visionary Strategies are Needed." *USA Today* (J. of Public Affairs). November 1994, pp 22 –25.

See: Ziegenfuss, J.T. "Building Country and Community Health Systems: The Futures and Systems Redesign Approach." Presented Madrid, Spain 1998. Monograph Award. Center for Latin American Public Administration. Caracas, Venezuela.

Questions: Are we able to use strategic planning concepts to assist our political leaders and citizens to weigh various options for country level directions, destinations and decisions?

EPILOGUE: THE STRATEGY SYSTEM AUDIT

All strategic planning and strategy formation systems, like all organizations, are in need of continuous improvement. One way to assess your current system's status is to conduct an audit.

In brief form, these lessons can be used as a checklist to guide the auditing of the planning system. Each of the items on the checklist is given a grade indicating whether that lesson has been learned by your team. Have each of the members of the planning group grade the organization from A for excellent to F for failure. Open discussion of strengths and weaknesses will expand the analysis.

If there is an interest in shortening the grading list, have each of the planning participants select critical items from the different types of lessons. For example, four or five items from each set of lessons would be selected for your organization's planning system review.

- Philosophy and concept
- Design and methods
- Progress outcomes and benefits

The exercise critiques your planning and strategy system design and is detailed enough to provide feedback on how you might improve over time. Used with constructive intent, the formative nature of the feedback will lead to redesign, not just judgment driven by discomfort.

To further support the design and redesign of strategy formation and planning systems, the Appendix includes five resources: (A) general model of strategic planning and formation; (B) vision building questions; (C) seven strategic planning consultant roles; (D) leading books on strategic planning; and (E) selected articles—recommended reading.

APPENDIX A

GENERAL MODEL OF
STRATEGY PLANNING AND FORMATION

• *External Analysis*. A review of external trends and issues such as technology, education, politics, economics and demographics in a search for threats and opportunities. This review is also made industry specific. Competitor analysis can be included here.

• *Internal Review*. An analysis of the strengths and weaknesses of the organization including its primary products and services, structure, management and culture. Core competencies are defined.

• *Vision Formulation*. Creative development of a scenario of the future. "Broad brush" at first, the vision becomes increasingly detailed to include products, services, size, location, markets and core values and assumptions.

• *Mission Design/Review*. Mission statements that evolve from the vision of a new company are designed. The existing mission is reviewed in light of the data developed from the external and internal reviews.

• *Gap Analysis*. The present organization and the future vision are compared to establish the points for action and to focus the management team on the differences.

• *Strategy Formulation*. Grand strategy is selected to guide the organization's decision-making processes. Concurrent and supportive strategies are also chosen.

• *Actions & Operational Objectives*. What must be done to attain the future is defined as primary initiating actions accompanied by a few key objectives that will begin movement toward the future.

• *Budget & Finances*. The vision and actions are translated into a financial plan for distributing resources to support the vision.

• *Evaluation Points & Milestones*. Points of plan review and milestones for measurement are created.

APPENDIX B

VISION BUILDING QUESTIONS

Visions are pushed out in iterations with general answers to the following. A first draft is "roughed out" with continuing discussions adding detail.

1. Why will our organization continue to exist in the next decade?

2. What changes do we expect in our core technologies and in our products and services? (new, obsolete, adaptive)?

3. How will we distribute or deliver our products and services differently?

4. How will our customers and clients change?

5. Will our geographic boundaries expand, shrink or maintain?

6. Where will we be located (headquarters, plants, branches)?

7. What will be the state of our physical plant (basic, luxurious, state-of-the-art)?

8. Who will staff our organization (types) and how many (more, less)?

9. How will we describe our structure (centralized, flat, hierarchical)?

10. What are our financial objectives (huge returns)?

11. What are the most important values and beliefs in our organization culture?

APPENDIX C

SEVEN STRATEGIC PLANNING CONSULTANT ROLES

1. Planning & Strategy Process Designer
   Consultant offers alternative designs for a planning and strategy formation process tailored to the unique needs of each organization. Design includes all major considerations from steps to data to participants.

2. Process Coach & Facilitator
   Consultant coaches planning participants through all phases of process, offering facilitation of group sessions, retreats and executive debates.

3. Data Collector
   Consultant helps to identify needed data for the process, offers methodologies for retrieving both quantitative and qualitative data and assists in or collects data through surveys, interviews, focus groups, official records analysis.

4. Research Analyst
   Consultant analyzes data for relevance to the strategy options, feeding back critical information to the participants.

5. Vision & Scenario Builder
   Consultant develops visions and scenarios for planners to consider. Drafts are developed independently or, most often, in collaboration with planning participants.

6. Options Identifier
   Consultant identifies strategy options for client, focusing on content alternatives such as growth, divestiture, merger, restructuring. The grand and operating strategies are debated by the clients.

7. Evaluator
   Consultant acts as evaluator of the strategic progress of the organization. Evaluation can be "formative" in that assistance forward is offered as a part of the strategy audit. Or, the evaluation can be "summative" as the strategic progress is *judged*.

APPENDIX D

BOOKS ON STRATEGIC PLANNING
A selection of these classic and current books could be used for academic courses and/or professional development and continuing education.

Ackoff, R.L. *A Concept of Corporate Planning*. Wiley, 1970 and *Creating the Corporate Future*. New York: Wiley 1981.

Lorange, P. (Editor) *Strategic Planning Process*. Aldershot, England: Dartmouth, 1994.

Mintzberg, H. *The Rise and Fall of Strategic Planning*. New York: Free Press, 1994.

Bryson, J.M. *Strategic Planning for Public and Nonprofit Organizations*. 3rd Edition. San Francisco: Jossey Bass, 2004.

Hamel, G.; Prahalad, C.K. *Competing for the Future*. Boston: Harvard Business School Press, 1994.

Kaplan, R. S.; Norton, D.P. *The Balanced Scorecard*. Boston: Harv. Bus School Press, 1996.

Kaplan, R.S. : Norton, D.P. *The Strategy Focused Organization*. Boston Harv. Bus. School Press, 2001.

Cummings, S.; Wilson, D. (Eds.). *Images of Strategy*. Oxford: Blackwell, 2003.

Ackerman, F.; Eden, C. *The Practice of Making Strategy: A Step by Step Guide*. Thousand Oaks, Ca.: Sage, 2005

Gruenig, R.; Kuehn, R. *Process Based Strategic Plans*. Frankfurt: Springer Verlag, 2005.

Allison, M.; Kaye, J. *Strategic Planning for Nonprofit Organizations: A Practical Guide and Workbook*. Hoboken, N.J. Wiley, 2005.

Hrebiniak, L.G. *Making Strategy Work: Leading Effective Execution and Change*. Upper Saddle River, N.J.: Wharton School Pub., 2005.

APPENDIX E

SELECTED ARTICLES RECOMMENDED READING
A selection of these articles could be used for academic courses and/ or professional development and continuing education.

Ackoff, R.L. "The Circular Organization Design: An Update." *Academy of Management Executive*. 3; 1989, 11-16.

Analoui, F.; Karami, A. "CEOs and Development of the Meaningful Mission Statement." *Corporate Governance*. 2(3); 2002; pp 13-20.

Bernick, C.L. "When Your culture needs a Makeover." *Harv. Bus. Rev*. 79(6); June 2001; pp 53-61.

Berry, F.S. "Innovation in Public Management: The Adoption of Strategic Planning." *Pub. Admin. Rev.* 54(4); 1994; pp 322-.

Berry, F.S.; Wechsler, B. "State Agencies' Experience with Strategic Planning: Findings from a National Survey." *Pub Admin Rev*. 55(2); 1995; pp 159-.

Bruton, G.D. "Strategic Public Planning: External Orientations and Strategic Planning Team Members." *Amer. Rev. Pub. Admin*. 23(4); 1983, 307-317.

Brody, S.D. Godschalk, D.R.; Burby, R.J. "Mandating citizen participation in plan making: Six Strategic Planning Choices" *J. Amer. Plan. Assn*. 69(3); Summer 2003, pp 245-

Collins, J.C.; Porras, J.I. "Building a Visionary Company." *California Management Review*. 37(2); Winter 1995; 80-100.

Courtney, C. Kirkland, J. Viguerie, P. "Strategy under Uncertainty." *Harv. Bus. Rev*. Nov.Dec, 1997.

Daake, D.; Dawley, D.D.; Anthony, W.P. "Formal Data Use in Strategic Planning: An Organizational Field Experiment." *J. Mgmt. Issues*. 16(2); Summer 2004, pp. 232-247.

Doeee, J. "Strategy as Options on the Future" *Sloan Mgmt. Rev*. Spring 1999.

Eisenhardt, K.M. "Strategy as Simple Rules." *Harv. Bus. Rev*. vol. 79, issue 1, p. 106. Jan 2001.

Eitel, D. F.; "Strategic Planning in Illinois: A State at the Crossroads." *Intl. J. Org Theory and Behavior*. 6(4); Winter 2003, pp 577-611.

Gavetti, G.; Rykin, J.W. "How Strategists really Think." *Harv. Bus. Rev*. Vol. 83, Issue 4, p. 54, April 2005.

Hall, M.J.; Lawson, J. "Using the Baldrige Criteria to assess Strategic Planning: A Case Study." *J. Quality and Participation.* 26(2); Summer 2003, pp 36-39.

Iansiti, M.; Levien, R. "Strategy as Ecology." *Harv. Bus. Rev.* Vol. 82, Issue 3, p. 68, March 2004.

Kaplan, R.S.; Norton, D.P. "Having Trouble with your Strategy? Then Map It." *Harv. Bus. Rev.* vol 78 issue 5, p 167, Sept/Oct 2000.

Landry, J.T. "The Art of the Adventure: 36 strategies to Seize the Competitive Edge." *Harv. Bus. Rev.* Vol. 82, Issue 3, p. 26, March 2004.

Leahy, T. "Bringing Elegance to Strategic Plans." *Business Finance.* June 2002.

Lovallo, D.; Kahneman, D. "How to take the outside view." *Harv. Bus. Rev.* Vol 81 Issue 7, p 62, July 2003.

Meeker, H. "Hands-On Futurism. How to Run a Scanning Project." *Futurist.* May-June 1993; 22-26.

Martin, R. "Changing the Mind of the Corporation." *Harv. Bus. Review.* Nov-Dec, 1993.

Mintzberg, H. "The Fall and Rise of Strategic Planning." *Harv. Bus. Review.* Jan-Feb 1994, 107-114.

Moyer, D. "The Sin in Synergy." *Harv. Bus. Rev.* Vol. 82, Issue 3, p. 131, March 2004.

Ohmae, K. "Getting Back to Strategy." *Harv. Bus. Review.* Nov-Dec, 1988.

Ozbekhan, H. "The Future of Paris: A Systems Study in Strategic Urban Planning." *Philosophical Transactions Royal Society London.* 287; 1977; 523-544.

Prahalad, C.K.; Hamel, G. "The Core Competencies of the Corporation." *Harv. Bus. Review.* May-June 1990, 79-91.

Rangan, V.K. "Lofty Missions, Down to Earth Plans" *Harv. Bus. Rev.* March 2004; pp. 112-119.

Stewart, J.M. "Future State VisioningCA Powerful Leadership Process." *Long Range Planning.* 26; December 1993; 89-98.

Stopford, J. "Should Strategy Makers Become Dream Weavers?" *Harv. Bus. Rev.* vol 28 iss 1, p. 165, Jan 2001. Wilson, I. "Realizing the Power of Strategic Vision." *Long Range Planning.* 25(5); 1992; 18-28.

Weitekamp, M.R.; Thorndyke, L.E.; Evarts, C.M. "Strategic Planning for Academic Health Centers." *Amer. J. Med.* 101, Sept. 1996; pp 309-315.

Ziegenfuss, J.T. "Are you Growing Systems Thinking Managers? Use a Systems Model to Teach and Practice Organizational Analysis and Planning, Policy and Development." *Systems Practice*. 5(5); 1992; 509-527.

INDEX

ABOUT THE AUTHOR

James T. Ziegenfuss, Jr., Ph.D., is Professor of Management & Health Care Systems in the Graduate Programs in Health & Public Administration, School of Public Affairs, Pennsylvania State University.

Appointed to the faculty in 1983, Professor Ziegenfuss teaches courses in strategic planning, health systems, quality management, organization behavior, and organization/ management consulting and coordinates the non-profit and human resources certificates. He holds the Ph.D. in Social Systems Sciences from the Wharton School of the University of Pennsylvania and masters' degrees in Psychology (Temple) and Public Administration (Penn State) and the B.A. in English (Maryland). At the Penn State Medical College he is Adjunct Professor of Medicine (1988–), co-directed the physician fellowship program in quality and has been Evaluation Coordinator for the six-year organization change project sponsored by Robert Wood Johnson/Pew (Redesigning Patient Care Systems).

While attending graduate school, he worked full time from 1973-83 in organization analysis and planning, including consulting evaluations, strategic planning at the single and multi-institutional levels, organizational change projects, and research and development of health care systems.

Dr. Ziegenfuss has written over 100 articles for journals and conferences and has authored ten books including, *The Organizational Path to Health Care Quality,* (1993), *Relearning Strategic Planning (1996); Organization & Management Problem Solving: A Systems & Consulting Approach* (Sage 2002) and his most recent edited works: *Portable Health Administration* with J. Sassani M.D. (Elsevier 2004) and *Core Curriculum for Medical Quality Management* with ACMQ physicians (Jones & Bartlett 2005). His monograph, "Country and Community Health Systems: The Futures and Systems Redesign Approach" was presented in Madrid and won top prize in the Latin American 1998 international manuscript competition. The paper was translated to Spanish and published by the Pan American Health Organization in 1999. Dr. Ziegenfuss received the distinguished service award from the American College of Medical Quality in 1999 for his contributions in education and research and has been Associate Editor of the *American Journal of Medical Quality* since 1989. Another prize monograph, "Building Citizen

Participation: The Purposes, Tools and Impact of Involvement" was published in 2000 by the Center for Latin American Administrative Reform. In 2004, he received the Regents Award for Senior Health Care Executives for leadership and management (American College of Healthcare Executives). At the annual meeting in Baden Baden, Germany in 2005, he was elected Fellow of the International Institute for Advanced Studies in Systems Research & Cybernetics for his innovative research contributions to health care systems and medicine.

Professor Ziegenfuss' current teaching, research and consulting interests are in the fields of strategic planning, quality management/customer service, and organizational development, particularly design and facilitation of strategic planning processes. He is finishing research on the design of customer friendly organizations for a new book. He is an active consultant to public and private organizations; his education, research, and consulting work has been supported by more than 75 organizations, including medical schools, associations, hospitals, banks and non-profit organizations.

Contact: telephone: 717-948-6053.... Email jtz1@psu.edu